THE

INVISIBLE

LADDER

THE
INVISIBLE
LADDER

An Anthology of Contemporary
American Poems for Young Readers

WITH THE POETS' OWN PHOTOS AND COMMENTARY

EDITED BY LIZ ROSENBERG

HENRY HOLT AND COMPANY · NEW YORK

To all the young readers who helped
To the poets who contributed so generously
And to Marc Aronson, a light in my mind and editor extraordinaire

Henry Holt and Company, Inc.
Publishers since 1866
115 West 18th Street
New York, New York 10011

Henry Holt is a registered
trademark of Henry Holt and Company, Inc.

Published in Canada by Fitzhenry & Whiteside Ltd.,
195 Allstate Parkway, Markham, Ontario L3R 4T8.

Library of Congress Cataloging-in-Publication Data
The invisible ladder: an anthology of contemporary American poems for
young readers / edited by Liz Rosenberg.
p.   cm.
Includes index.
Summary: Features such poets as Robert Bly, Allen Ginsberg, Nikki
Giovanni, and Galway Kinnell by including photos, selections of
their work, and comments on their poetry.
1. Young adult poetry, American.   2. American poetry—20th
century—History and criticism —Theory, etc.   3. Poets,
American—20th century—Biography.   4. American poetry 20th
century.   5. Family—Juvenile poetry.   6. Poetry—Authorship.
[1. American poetry—Collections.   2. Poets, American.]   I. Rosenberg, Liz.
PS586.3.I45   1996   811'.5408—dc20   96-12361

ISBN 0-8050-3836-1
First Edition—1996

Printed in the United States of America
on acid-free paper. ∞
3   5   7   9   10   8   6   4
Book design by Debbie Glasserman

C O N T E N T S

Introduction 3

MARVIN BELL
Statement 7
Being in Love 8
Dew at the Edge of a Leaf 9
To Dorothy 10
From *Who & Where* 11
The Mystery of Emily Dickinson 12
White Clover 13

MOLLY BENDALL
Statement 17
The Need for Shoes 19

ROBERT BLY
Statement 21
Seeing the Eclipse in Maine 22
As a Child 23
Things My Brother and I Could Do 24
*Listening to a Cricket in
    the Wainscoting* 25
In a Train 25

DAVID CHIN
Statement 27
Sleeping Father 28
Sterling Williams' Nosebleed 29

VIC COCCIMIGLIO
Statement 33
*St. Francis Speaks to Me at a
    Young Age* 34
Night Beach 35

ROBERT CREELEY
Statement 37
Something for Easter 38

V

CONTENTS

ROBERT CREELEY *In a Boat Shed* 39
 The Rain 40

RITA DOVE Statement 43
 Centipede 44

CORNELIUS EADY Statement 47
 Crows in a Strong Wind 48
 Johnny Laces Up His Red Shoes 49
 The View from the Roof,
  Waverly Place 51

MARTÍN ESPADA Statement 53
 Courthouse Graffiti for Two Voices 54
 Tires Stacked in the Hallways of
  Civilization 55
 Who Burns for the Perfection
  of Paper 56

TESS GALLAGHER Statement 59
 Unsteady Yellow 60

MARIA MAZZIOTTI GILLAN Statement 63
 In New Jersey Once 64

ALLEN GINSBERG Statement 67
 Fourth Floor, Dawn, Up All Night
  Writing Letters 68

NIKKI GIOVANNI Statement 71
 The World Is Not a Pleasant Place
  to Be 72

VI

ANDREW HUDGINS   Statement 75
                        Childhood of the Ancients 76
                        Tree 77
                        The Air 78

MILTON KESSLER   Statement 81
                        Waxwings 82

GALWAY KINNELL   Statement: Childhood Music 85
                        Blackberry Eating 88
                        Another Night in the Ruins 89

CAROLYN KIZER   Statement 93
                        The Great Blue Heron 94

TED KOOSER   Statement 97
                        Myrtle 98

MAXINE KUMIN   Statement 101
                        The Retrieval System 102

STANLEY KUNITZ   Statement 105
                        The Portrait 106
                        After the Last Dynasty 107

GREG KUZMA   Statement 111
                        Night Things 112
                        Ice Skating 113

LI-YOUNG LEE   Statement 115
                        Eating Together 116
                        I Ask My Mother to Sing 117

HEATHER McHUGH   Statement 119

VII

HEATHER McHUGH   *A Night in a World* 120

KYOKO MORI   Statement 123
                       Barbie Says Math Is Hard 124

SHARON OLDS   Statement 127
                       The Race 129

LINDA PASTAN   Statement 133
                       Egg 134
                       September 135

DIANA RIVERA   Statement 137
                       Under the Apple Tree 138
                       Dinner Together 141

LIZ ROSENBERG   Statement 143
                       Which One Is the Grown-up?
                          Haiku 144
                       No Boundaries 144
                       They Are Planning to Cancel the School
                          Milk Program to Fund a Tax Cut for
                          the Middle Class 145

DAVID ST. JOHN   Statement 147
                       Guitar 148

MAURYA SIMON   Statement 151
                       Night 152
                       Standing Between Two Ideas 153

W. D. SNODGRASS   Statement 155
                       From *Snow Songs* 156

VIII

GERALD STERN   Statement 159
                      Royal Manor Road 160
                      Behaving Like a Jew 161
                      From *Lucky Life* 162

RUTH STONE   Statement 165
                      The Nose 166

LUCIEN STRYK   Statement 169
                      Dawn 170

ALICE WALKER   Statement 173
                      Remember? 174

JANE O. WAYNE   Statement 177
                      By Accident 178
                      The Eavesdropper 179
                      Cleaning Indian Dahl 180
                      In Praise of Zigzags 181

DIETER WESLOWSKI   Statement 183
                      Dry World 184
                      Zoe and the Ghosts 184
                      Heart 185
                      Pablo, 185

ROBLEY WILSON   Statement 187
                      Envoi 188
                      I Wish in the City of Your Heart 189

Ways to Use This Book 191
Biographical Notes 197
Index of First Lines 209

IX

THE

INVISIBLE

LADDER

INTRODUCTION

In writing this introduction, the voices of the poets in this book come back to me: "I write poetry because I am *alone*" (Vic Coccimiglio). "I read poems as if they were letters written to me, and I wrote poems back as answers" (Linda Pastan). "I knew as a child that no one knew me . . ." (Li-Young Lee). "Children should listen to poets; poets should listen to them!" (Gerald Stern).

Young people deserve great poetry; great poetry deserves young readers. Because I did not find in any anthology of poems the book I was hoping for, I made my own. There are many fine books of children's poems for children—Shel Silverstein's and Dr. Seuss's are among our best—but this thing, "children's poetry," is its own kind of creature. It is not the only kind of poetry there is. The poetry I liked best as a child was not children's poetry but poetry, period. It was poetry that grew along with me. I loved Robert Frost and Carl Sandburg, Edna St. Vincent Millay and, a little later on, Sylvia Plath and Robert Lowell—and I still do. I think I needed, even then, to know that real poets were alive and well, and writing in the world.

Most poetry anthologies for young readers are either what I call peanut-butter-and-jelly anthologies—books full of bouncy rhymes too stupid for any adult to put up with (as if children were tone-deaf or didn't know any better)—or poems by the dead and the very dead. In too many collections of poems for young readers, you never encounter a poem by a living poet who does not write in a children's poetry ghetto. Two beautiful and, for me, inspirational exceptions are Paul Janeczko's anthologies for older young readers and Kenneth Koch's *Rose, Where Did You Get That Red?* I'm sure there are others.

Poetry is a kind of a code; it takes patience and practice to learn how to break the code, and besides, you have to love the thrill of decoding

3

itself. Not everyone loves poetry. Not everyone HAS to. Yet poetry, as little as it is known or loved in this country, manages to thrive everywhere. There are poets living in every corner of America—in Alaska and New England and the South, the Midwest, and Hawaii. There are black poets, Native American poets, Latino poets, women and men poets, young and old poets.

This book contains many kinds of poems aimed at many kinds of readers. But I think most will probably skim through and take what they like as they find it. You may stop at a poem because of the title, or because you like the poet's face, or because you are drawn to what a poet has written about poetry or childhood. I wanted the poets' faces to be here—both as adults and as children—because all poets, including the great ones, were once children. I want to make it very clear that poetry is possible. Anyone can become a poet at any age.

It seems to me that any one of the poems in this anthology might trigger serious and lively conversations, and serious and lively poems. (See "Ways to Use This Book" at the back of the book.) You might read a poem like Maria Gillan's "In New Jersey Once" and think about your own hometown, really look at it. You can sketch it, or take a photograph of it, to help you see it more clearly. Or you could write a poem about any place that you love—or a secret place you often escape to—or think of a place as being alive. What might it say to us? Or write a poem that imagines what something was like a long, long time ago. All this from a single poem!

Poetry helps us to focus on the world, to focus more clearly on what is inside ourselves and all around us. "Who are you? What are you?" a stranger once asked the Buddha, and he answered, "I am awake." The poet's job is to remain awake even when the rest of the world appears to be sleepwalking. In my experience, young people are more often awake than adults. They feel things and think about things keenly.

And, like all of us, they look for a fresh language to help put those thoughts and feelings into words. I hope that some of these poems will spark a recognition—the aha! of a friend unexpectedly met, familiar and surprising at the same time.

Galway Kinnell writes in his note in this book: "When I found the world of poets, I realized I was not so odd after all. And when, one day, a teacher mentioned that Robert Frost was living and writing on a farm only a few hundred miles north of Pawtucket, I realized that poetry was not an extinct art, that poets could still exist in the world. And I started to write poetry."

It doesn't matter what you love to do—repair bicycles, run long distance, pray, cook, play catch, write poems. The important thing is to do it, as well as you can. The poet Rainer Maria Rilke wrote, "You must change your life." We may as well begin now.

5

MARVIN BELL

Like most young people in the small town in which I grew up, I went through high school thinking that poetry was written in the language of earlier times, expressing flowery sentiments in ways certain to embarrass any red-blooded American boy or girl. I was wrong.

Well, of course I should have realized that poetry can be modern because popular music is always modern. The words of songs are a kind of poetry, and I knew lots of songs.

Writing poetry is always about being young, because each poem is a fresh beginning, a new world of words to explore, a chance for surprise or a miracle. Writing is a kind of play, even when the subject is serious.

Also, we never lose our sense of childhood. That is the time when we begin to notice how we feel. Poetry finds words for what life feels like, and feelings have staying power.

1

BEING IN LOVE

with someone who is not in love with
you, you understand my predicament.
Being in love with you, who are not
in love with me, you understand my dilemma.
Being in love with your being in love
with me, which you are not, you understand

the difficulty. Being in love with your
being, you can well imagine how hard it is.
Being in love with your being you,
no matter you are not your being being in
love with me, you can appreciate and pity
being in love with you. Being in love

with someone who is not in love, you know
all about being in love when being in love
is being in love with someone who is not
in love being with you, which is
being in love, which you know only too well,
Love, being in love with being in love.

DEW AT THE EDGE OF A LEAF

The broader leaves collect
enough to see early
by a wide spread of moonlight,
and they shine!, shine!—
who are used to turning
faces to the light.

Looking up is farthest.
From here or under any tree,
I know what will transpire:
leaves in their watery halos have
an overhead-to-underfoot career,
and thrive toward falling.

In a passage of time and water,
I am halfway—a leaf in July?
In August? I take no pity.
Everything green is turning brown,
it's true, but then too
everything turning brown is green.

9

TO DOROTHY

You are not beautiful, exactly.
You are beautiful, inexactly.
You let a weed grow by the mulberry
and a mulberry grow by the house.
So close, in the personal quiet
of a windy night, it brushes the wall
and sweeps away the day till we sleep.

A child said it, and it seemed true:
"Things that are lost are all equal."
But it isn't true. If I lost you,
the air wouldn't move, nor the tree grow.
Someone would pull the weed, my flower.
The quiet wouldn't be yours. If I lost you,
I'd have to ask the grass to let me sleep.

FROM WHO & WHERE

2

Who I am is a short person with small feet
and fingers. When the hill is snowy,
I have to walk on the grass, and this gives
me a different viewpoint and wet shoes.
I see writers grow huge
in their writings. I get smaller yet,
so small that sometimes a tree is more
than I can look up to. I am down here with
all the other tiny, weak things. Sure,
once in a while I pull myself up
to assert something to the air, but oftener
I look for what was lost in the weeds.
The Gods drink nectar, I drink fruit juice.
All my life, people have told me,
"You are big, or will be." But I'm small.
I am not at the center of the circle.
I am not part of the ring. Like you,
I am not the core, the dark star or the lit star.
I take a step. The wind takes a step.
I take a drink of water. The earth swallows.
I just live here—like you, like you, like you.

THE MYSTERY OF EMILY DICKINSON

Sometimes the weather goes on for days
but you were different. You were divine.
While the others wrote more and longer,
you wrote much more and much shorter.
I held your white dress once: 12 buttons.
In the cupola, the wasps struck glass
as hard to escape as you hit your sound
again and again asking Welcome. No one.

Except for you, it were a trifle:
This morning, not much after dawn,
in level country, not New England's,
through leftovers of summer rain I
went out rag-tag to the curb, only
a sleepy householder at his routine
bending to trash, when a young girl
in a white dress your size passed,

so softly!, carrying her shoes. It must be
she surprised me—her barefoot quick-step
and the earliness of the hour, your dress—
or surely I'd have spoken of it sooner.
I should have called to her, but a neighbor
wore that look you see against happiness.
I won't say anything would have happened
unless there was time, and eternity's plenty.

12

WHITE CLOVER

Once when the moon was out about three-quarters
and the fireflies who are the stars
of backyards
were out about three-quarters
and about three-fourths of all the lights
in the neighborhood
were on because people can be at home,
I took a not so innocent walk
out among the lawns,
navigating by the light of lights,
and there there were many hundreds of moons
on the lawns
where before there was only polite grass.
These were moons on long stems,
their long stems giving their greenness
to the center of each flower
and the light giving its whiteness to the tops
of the petals. I could say
it was light from stars
touched the tops of flowers and no doubt
something heavenly reaches what grows outdoors
and the heads of men who go hatless,
but I like to think we have a world
right here, and a life
that isn't death. So I don't say it's better
to be right here. I say this is where

13

many hundreds of core-green moons
gigantic to my eye
rose because men and women had sown green grass,
and flowered to my eye in man-made light,
and to some would be as fire in the body
and to others a light in the mind
over all their property.

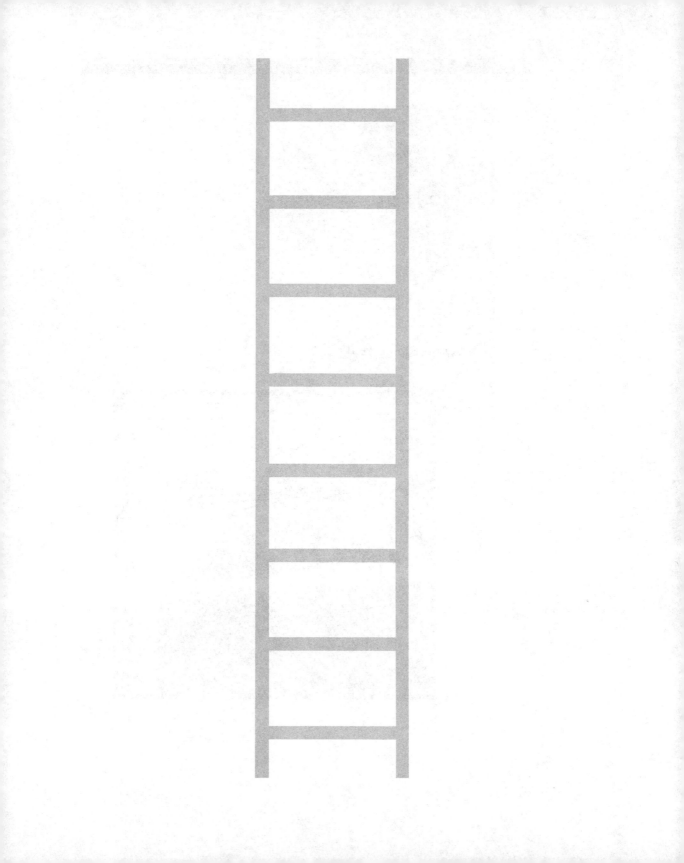

MOLLY BENDALL

I was fortunate enough to have a mother who loved reading poems to my brother and me from the time we were quite small. The rhythms of a human voice and the emotion brought with them had a lasting effect and continue to inspire me. I think, even then, I understood the strange combination of solace and refuge found in that space of the poem as well as the mystery and vastness in much of the language and subject matter.

One of my favorites was Christina Rossetti's "Who Has Seen the Wind?"

> Who has seen the wind?
>   Neither I nor you;
> But when the leaves hang trembling,
>   The wind is passing through
>
> Who has seen the wind?
>   Neither you nor I;
> But when the trees
>   Bow down their heads,
> The wind is passing by.

Though at first this poem may seem to attempt an explanation of nature's forces, I'm always struck by the fact that the wind remains defiant and refuses to be pinned down. Other favorites I feel compelled to mention, especially now that I've begun reading them to my daughter, include: Vachel Lindsay's "The Moon's the North Wind's Cooky"; Harold Monro's "Overheard on a Saltmarsh"; Mary Leslie Newton's "Queen Anne's Lace"; Bliss Carman's "A Vagabond Song"; and many poems by Edward Lear, Eugene Field, Rose Fyleman, and Walter de la Mare.

THE NEED FOR SHOES

One afternoon in her loft
the girl reaches in the closet
for her huaraches
and slides each hand under the woven straps
caressing the slopes
of the blackened insteps.
Her hands make them
dance the mazurka.

Another girl sleeps
with her work shoes on
in the dry hay of a barn.
Later she slips them off and
holds the moist leather soles,
while the mare's breath
reaches over her shoulder.

The girl changes the rhythm
to a polka and stamps it out
against the hardwood floor,
as though it were a secret finally disclosed.
In the downstairs apartment a third girl,
seated at the dinner table,
looks up from her plate to listen.

ROBERT BLY

We all wrote poetry when we were children. So when reporters used to ask Bill Stafford why he wrote poetry, he might reply, "Well, that's not really the question: the question is, why did you stop?" My mother loved poetry, and she came from a long line of people in Norway who wrote poems for the newspapers. I had a teacher in high school that we all fell in love with, and she would recite poetry. I remember thinking to myself, If she likes poetry, it can't be all bad, so I ignored what the others thought and kept up a secret love of it.

SEEING THE ECLIPSE IN MAINE

It started about noon. On top of Mount Batte,
We were all exclaiming. Someone had a cardboard
And a pin, and we all cried out when the sun
Appeared in tiny form on the notebook cover.

It was hard to believe. The high school teacher
We'd met called it a pinhole camera,
People in the Renaissance loved to do that.
And when the moon had passed partly through

We saw on a rock underneath a fir tree,
Dozens of crescents—made the same way—
Thousands! Even our straw hats produced
A few as we moved them over the bare granite.

We shared chocolate, and one man from Maine
Told a joke. Suns were everywhere—at our feet.

AS A CHILD

I was one of the saved.
The chickens were, too.
I didn't know about my brother,
But stones had *something*.

Each morning came; only
The hired girl was ready.
The rest of us dozed,
And got up, and fed chickens.

The guinea hens rose
From unimaginable places.
Every step they took
They made new air.

We were all saved.
We gathered eggs.
They slept in trees
And had better nights.

THINGS MY BROTHER AND I COULD DO
For W.S.

Well there's no end of things to do.

We could go out and catch gophers.
We could read books.
We could pick the mud off tractor tires.

We could think about a pheasant falling.
We could think about Father falling.
We could see where he fell.

It was late one night, and he fell down
And hit his head on a boot scraper—
He didn't die—saying good-bye to others.

We could wonder about the War.
We could think about Bertha, who did die.
We could think about her daughter, who lived with us.

We could think about why her face was so thin.

LISTENING TO A CRICKET IN THE WAINSCOTING

That sound of his is like a boat with black sails.
Or a widow under a redwood tree, warning
passersby that the tree is about to fall.
Or a bell made of black tin in a Mexican village.
Or the hair in the ear of a hundred-year-old man!

25

IN A TRAIN

There has been a light snow.
Dark car tracks move in out of the darkness.
I stare at the train window marked with soft dust.
I have awakened at Missoula, Montana, utterly happy.

DAVID CHIN

I first began to write poetry when I was around eleven or twelve although I didn't know at that time that it was poetry. What I was writing then seemed to be a collection of drawings, doodles, private jokes for sharing with a few friends, and sometimes my reactions to the often incomprehensible and absurd rules of school. Later on, as a teenager, I discovered the music and lyrics of Bob Dylan, especially the notes on the back of his albums, and was captivated not only by what he said but by how he said it. This discovery led me into the world of poetry.

SLEEPING FATHER

My father sits in his chair and snores.
Inhaling, he rasps like an anchor chain
rattling off a ship, dropping into the sea.
When he exhales, waves hiss on distant shores.

In his dream, he carries the kite
his uncle made for him and walks the village path
thinking of his father who sailed for America years ago.
I wonder if it has to be this way with fathers.

As he sleeps with his head tipped back,
his mouth half open, behind shut eyelids
the frailest of objects climbs the sky
and a string slides through his fingers.

STERLING WILLIAMS' NOSEBLEED

Sterling Williams has a nosebleed.
Sterling Williams of the cow's tail.
Miss Alidyce called him the cow's tail,
the cow's tail after eight forty-five AM.
Sterling Williams with the incredible swagger.
Sterling Williams who'd flush the toilet
in the boy's room at P.S. 24 over and over
until clean water began to pour
over the edge of the bowl.
Sterling Williams who'd drink that water on a dare
and prove we were all "chickenshit."
Sterling Williams has a nosebleed.
Sterling Williams who could turn his eyelids inside out
and leave them that way forever.
Sterling Williams the black kid.
Sterling Williams who knew everything worth knowing.
Sterling Williams who could gouge your spinning top
squinting one eye on the throw.
Sterling Williams has a nosebleed.
Sterling Williams with brown clay
rolled into a foot long snake
dangling out of his unzipped pants.
Sterling Williams who could swagger
swaying the dangling clay back and forth.
Sterling Williams has a nosebleed.
Sterling Williams from the wrong side of Hudson Boulevard,
the wrong side of Bergen Avenue,

the wrong side of Jackson Avenue,
the wrong side of the world beyond Jackson Avenue.
Sterling Williams has a nosebleed.
Sterling Williams who drank watercolor rinse water
to prove it was non-toxic.
Sterling Williams who seized every second
Miss Alidyce was somewhere else.
Sterling Williams who taught me how
to make my armpits fart.
Sterling Williams has a nosebleed.
Sterling Williams has a nosebleed—
the blood pours out
all over his white shirt.
Sterling Williams whose parents
have to meet with Miss Alidyce
and Mr. Benway the principal.
Drops of Sterling's blood fall
on the smooth yellow third grade desk.
Miss Alidyce runs for the wet rag.
Miss Alidyce holds Sterling's head way back.
Miss Alidyce who has jewelry
and a brown leather cover for the attendance book.
Sterling Williams has a nosebleed.
The class watches Miss Alidyce pinch Sterling's nose.
Sterling's blood flecks the floor.
Sterling's blood drips from Miss Alidyce's bracelet.
Sterling's blood drips from Miss Alidyce's elbow.
Sterling Williams shows us he knows how to bleed.
Miss Alidyce has to go for ice.

Sterling on the verge of tears.
Sterling who has found Miss Alidyce's last straw.
Sterling gives us a sidelong glance.
Sterling shrugs his shoulders and fakes a smile.
Sterling Williams the scapegoat
condemned to act out for the class.
Sterling Williams has a nosebleed.
The tragic suspended and resuspended
Sterling Williams who could make me laugh
    uncontrollably
even in front of Miss Alidyce.
Sterling Williams who never had a chance.
Sterling Williams.

VIC COCCIMIGLIO

I write poetry because I am *alone*. Being alone has nothing to do with being lonely. In my solitude, I attempt to understand God.

The great Russian poet Marina Tsvetaeva wrote in her brilliant essay "History of a Dedication" (translated by Stephen Lottridge and Stephen Tapscott): "In the final analysis you write your way to God."

At 41, I struggle to believe in her words. I continue to write poetry.

ST. FRANCIS* SPEAKS
TO ME AT A YOUNG AGE

For hours I sat on our driveway beneath the dogwood tree. After spotting some chirping birds my older brother had shaken a branch, knocking a baby robin, soft as a pumpkin's flesh, out of an unprotected nest.

That featherless bird lay motionless on the cold concrete, closed eyes bulging beneath a tiny domed head. My father and brother exchanged glances, and when their eyes met my brother ran away. I knelt beside the bird, my face to the cement, but found no movement of breath.

When the mother robin returned to her nest she found one less mouth singing with emptiness. She chirped and chirped at me; and all that day I sat beneath the dogwood tree, trying to explain my brother's action, something he has long forgotten, something I still don't understand.

* St. Francis is the patron saint of birds.

NIGHT BEACH

I could just as easily be nine years old,
sitting on this beach at high noon,
waiting for my father to swim out to the buoy
and back; but here, neither child nor father,

I am alone, counting my breaths,
thinking about how my grandfather
used to count ants on the patio
while chanting: *I never kill them;*
I never destroy them. Let them live.

If he were still alive
he could be here with me,
and together we could count sandpipers
scuttling along the shore,
now that a new day is forming
as it must have
one hundred million years before we were born.

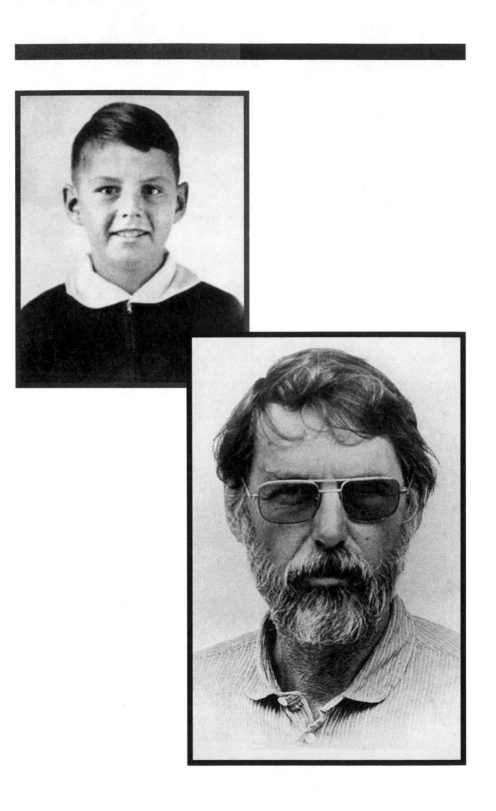

ROBERT CREELEY

I suppose one doesn't really locate childhood until it's gone, and then a sudden or slow recognition comes to make clear the poignance and particularity of that time in spite of its exceptional vulnerability and, very often, its pain. Perhaps it's that one will never be in the world again so completely, so specific to each thing there also. It is not simply that we grow up but that we move into shells of habit and function. Our bodies become mechanical. Our ways of thinking grow irritable. Nothing really happens again despite the chaos of wars and disintegrating cultures. We rationalize and move away.

As kids we were *here*. There was no other place to be, even in fantasy or those secret places invented for survival.

Herman Melville, the poet Charles Olson told me, had framed over his worktable the words "Be true to the dreams of thy youth. . . ." Such dreams will prove the source of your lives and make you human and real at last. Trust them.

SOMETHING FOR EASTER

I pulled the street up as you suggested
—and found what?

> 1 nickel
> 2 pieces gum

etc.

But we are practical
—but winter is long & however much one
does save, there is never
enough.

38

IN A BOAT SHED

I waited too long,
I waited for you forever and ever:

the changing unchanging restlessness
of the signs they didn't put up

or down; the boxes of oranges,
rat poisons, barns, a sled with no runners,

snow, refreshments, pineapples;
the odor of burnt wood, cigarettes

neither one of us should smoke,
but do—

I waited for you.

39

THE RAIN

All night the sound had
come back again,
and again falls
this quiet, persistent rain.

What am I to myself
that must be remembered,
insisted upon
so often? Is it

40

that never the ease,
even the hardness,
of rain falling
will have for me

something other than this,
something not so insistent—
am I to be locked in this
final uneasiness.

Love, if you love me,
lie next to me.
Be for me, like rain,
the getting out

of the tiredness, the fatuousness, the semi-
lust of intentional indifference.
Be wet
with a decent happiness.

RITA DOVE

Although I loved books, I had no aspirations to be a *writer*. I liked to *write* . . . and sometimes, on long summer days when I ran out of material to read, or my legs had fallen asleep because I had been curled up on the couch for hours on end, I invented my own stories.

Most were never finished. Those that were, I didn't show to anyone. I didn't think making up stories was something ordinary people admitted to doing. There were no living role models for me—a writer was a dead white male, usually with a long white beard to match.

Finally, in twelfth grade, I had a crucial experience. My English teacher, Miss Oechsner, took me to a book signing in a downtown hotel. She didn't ask me if I'd like to go—she got my parents' permission instead, signed me and another guy out of school one day (that other guy is a literature professor at Berkeley now, by the way), and took us to meet a REAL LIVE AUTHOR. He was John Ciardi, a poet who had translated Dante's *Divine Comedy,* which I had heard of, vaguely. That day I realized that writers were real people, and that it was possible to be a writer, to write down a poem or story in the intimate sphere of one's own room, and then share it with the world.

From Rita Dove, The Poet's World *(Washington, D.C.: Library of Congress, 1995). Reprinted by permission of the author.*

43

CENTIPEDE

With the storm moved on the next town
we take a flashlight down to the basement

Nested chairs stripped of varnish
Turpentine shadows stiff legs in the air

Look by the fusebox a centipede Dad says
I scream and let go of his hairy arm

44

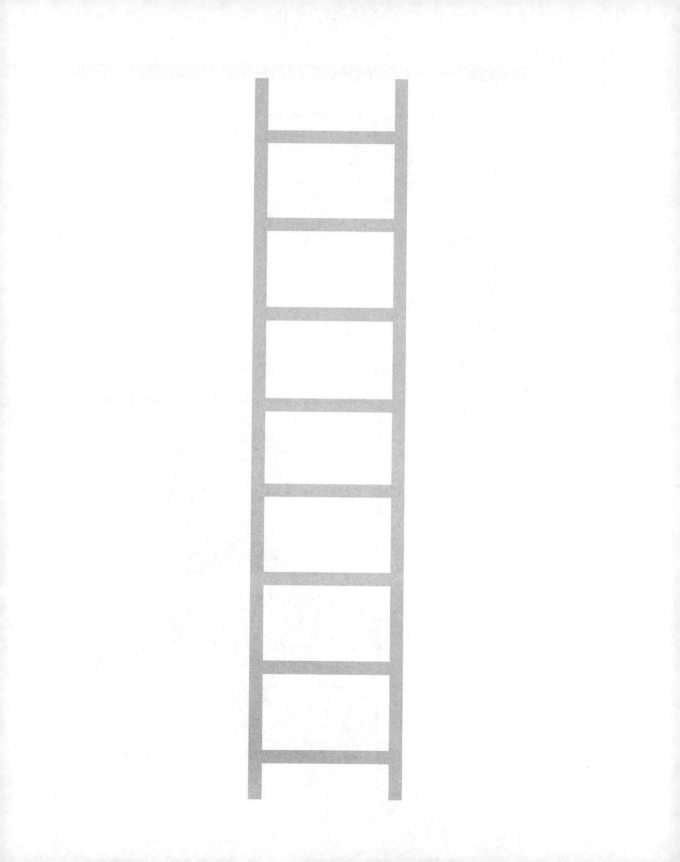

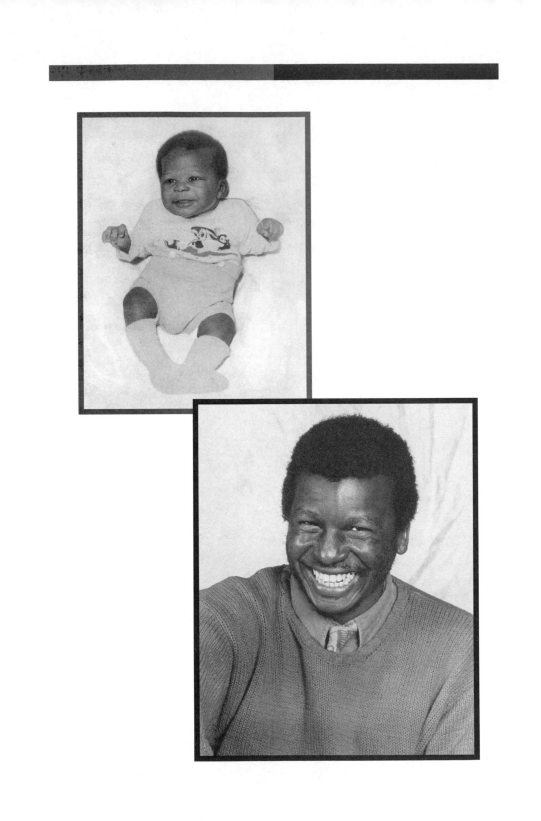

CORNELIUS EADY

As a child, I loved the library, but the books I enjoyed reading were things like the *Encyclopedia Britannica*. I loved reading articles and books about science: nuclear submarines, satellites.

While I do think that reading those books, so different from the world I would have to walk home to, probably helped in terms of poetic imagination and diction, I could just as easily make a case for the lyrics of the popular songs I was listening to over headphones in the library's AV department, or the unique ways my family and the people in my neighborhood used language. My mother used words like *stew-beef* (West Indian, I believe); my father, terms like *take big steps to save your shoes,* or *God's a gopher* (as in "If so and so did that . . ."). Later, I would find that exact phrase, something I thought invented by my father, in Zora Hurston's *Their Eyes Were Watching God.*

I think the best thing I was doing was building up the stories I would use later, when I was older, and lucky enough to run into the adults who would help me uncover the music lying just beneath the surface.

CROWS IN A STRONG WIND

Off go the crows from the roof.
The crows can't hold on.
They might as well
Be perched on an oil slick.

Such an awkward dance,
These gentlemen
In their spottled-black coats.
Such a tipsy dance,

As if they didn't know where they were.
Such a humorous dance,
As they try to set things right,
As the wind reduces them.

Such a sorrowful dance.
How embarrassing is love
When it goes wrong

In front of everyone.

JOHNNY LACES UP HIS RED SHOES

If Fred Astaire had been really smart,
He would have danced like Johnny dances on Friday night,
With his brilliant red shoes
That women can detect half a block away.

If Fred Astaire had been all he was cracked up to be,
He would have danced like Johnny dances on Friday night,
On two pools of quicksilver
Painted fire-engine red.

Johnny is lacing up his red shoes.
He is a pizza,
A kiss in the dark.
And as his fingers tie the laces,
He thinks of long, dark hair.

On his bitter-sweet sofa bed
Johnny is lacing up his red shoes,
And as his fingers tighten the laces,
His work clothes slide deeper
Into the evening shadows.

If Fred Astaire had been serious,
He would have walked through the door of the neighborhood bar
  like Johnny does on Friday night,
Wearing two small volcanos
That are permitted to erupt for only three nights.

THE VIEW FROM THE ROOF,
WAVERLY PLACE

By accident, I gaze at
These two young guys
Standing on the roof across
From my office window, a moment
Otherwise theirs. They watch
And listen to Sixth Avenue.
They talk. They have time
In their lives for a smoke.
Then the one on the left loops
His arm around the other's shoulder,
—*My buddy, my buddy.* They have
A quilt of lives spread below them,
The cool thrill of looking down.

MARTÍN ESPADA

My poetry is based on two foundations: the image, and the political imagination.

Although "image" in poetry refers to all five senses, I was influenced particularly by the work of my father, who is a documentary photographer. I think of myself as focusing a camera lens as I write, always striving to make the picture clearer, sharper, more detailed. I am a believer in metaphor and simile as methods of constructing these images. The image is to the poem what the boxcar is to the train. String enough boxcars together, and the poem begins to move.

Poetry of the political imagination is a matter of both vision and language. Any progressive social change must be imagined first, to move from vision to reality. Any oppressive social condition, before it can be changed, must be named and condemned in words that persuade by stirring the emotions, awakening the senses. This political imagination is present in all the poems presented here. It should be noted that the poems strive to go beyond protest: I am interested in the *artistry* of dissent. Poetry of the political imagination often involves *advocacy:* speaking on behalf of others who do not have the opportunity to be heard, a characteristic also illustrated in the poems found here.

COURTHOUSE GRAFFITI
FOR TWO VOICES

Jimmy C.
Greatest Car Thief Alive
Chelsea '88

Then what
are you doing
here?

TIRES STACKED IN THE HALLWAYS OF CIVILIZATION

—CHELSEA, MASSACHUSETTS

"Yes, Your Honor, there are rodents,"
said the landlord to the judge,
"but I let the tenant
have a cat. Besides,
he stacks his tires
in the hallway."

The tenant confessed
in stuttering English:
"Yes, Your Honor,
I am from El Salvador,
and I put my tires
in the hallway."

The judge puffed up
his robes
like a black bird
shaking off rain:
"Tires out of the hallway!
You don't live in a jungle
anymore. This
is a civilized country."

So the defendant was ordered
to remove his tires
from the hallways of civilization,
and allowed to keep the cat.

WHO BURNS FOR THE PERFECTION OF PAPER

At sixteen, I worked after high school hours
at a printing plant
that manufactured legal pads:
Yellow paper
stacked seven feet high
and leaning
as I slipped cardboard
between the pages,
then brushed red glue
up and down the stack.
No gloves: fingertips required
for the perfection of paper,
smoothing the exact rectangle.
Sluggish by 9 PM, the hands
would slide along suddenly sharp paper,
and gather slits thinner than the crevices
of the skin, hidden.
Then the glue would sting,
hands oozing
till both palms burned
at the punchclock.

Ten years later, in law school,
I knew that every legal pad
was glued with the sting of hidden cuts,
that every open lawbook
was a pair of hands
upturned and burning.

TESS GALLAGHER

I began to love words for their beauty and power, and the delicious taste they left in my mouth as a young girl growing up in the logging camps of the Olympic Peninsula, where my mother and father were loggers. I learned words could defend a person, could persuade, could call or dismiss. Sometimes I had to use them fiercely to defend my three brothers and myself from the gangs of boys who hounded us home from school. Later I learned how words caress and calm and invite and bind up our losses. One of my great subjects is kisses. At the start of my book, *Portable Kisses Expanded,* I say: "Ideally a reader should finish this book, then find somebody to kiss."

UNSTEADY YELLOW

I went to the field to break
and to bury my precious things.
I went to the field
with a sack and a spade,
to the cool field alone.

All that he gave me
I dashed and I covered.
The glass horse, the necklace,
the live bird with its song, with
its wings like two harps—
in the ground, in the damp ground.

Its song, when I snatched it again
to air, flung it with light
over the tall new corn, its pure joy
must have reached him.

In a day it was back, my freed bird
was back. Oh now, what will I do,
what will I do with its song
on my shoulder, with its heart
on my shoulder when we come to
the field, to the high yellow field?

MARIA MAZZIOTTI GILLAN

In my own poems, I try to combine plain, direct speech with a reverence for the beauty and music of language, hoping to create poems about the moment of understanding that we attain even in the midst of our ordinary lives.

One of the major themes in my work stems from my experience as a first-generation Italian American. I attempt to re-create the immigrant experience in America. I want to speak for all people who are outside the mainstream of American life, and who have traditionally been too poor and powerless to express themselves.

63

IN NEW JERSEY ONCE

In New Jersey once, marigolds grew wild.
Fields swayed with daisies.
Oaks stood tall on mountains.
Powdered butterflies graced the velvet air.

Listen. It was like that.
Before the bulldozers.
Before the cranes.
Before the cement sealed the earth.

64

Even the stars, which used to hang
in thick clusters in the black sky,
even the stars are dim.

Burrow under the blacktop,
under the cement, the old dark earth
is still there. Dig your hands into it,
feel it, deep, alive on your fingers.

Know that the earth breathes and pulses still.
Listen. It mourns. In New Jersey once, flowers grew.

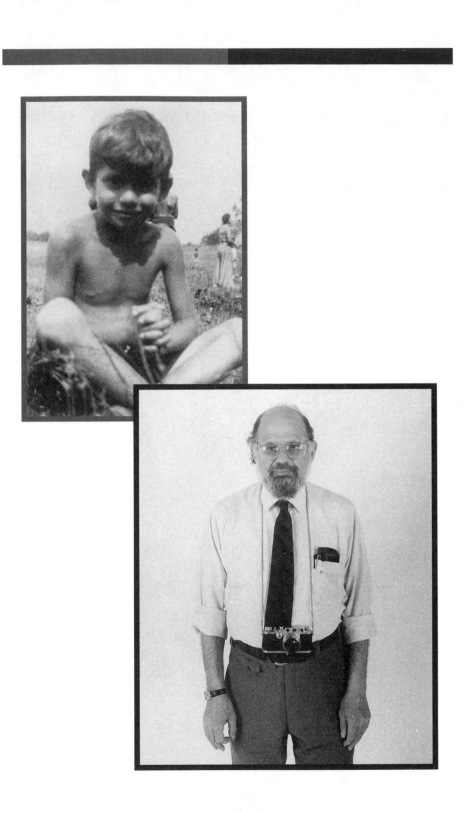

ALLEN GINSBERG

Great fat 300-pound Miss Frances Durbin, who had been to Paris with her long-time roommate Miss Wagner, sat in her classroom Eastside High School in 1942 Paterson, New Jersey, one afternoon before World War II in America, and read aloud verses from Walt Whitman's "Song of Myself" in so enthusiastic and joyous a voice, so confident and lifted with laughter, that I immediately understood "I wear my hat indoors as well as out. . . . Do I contradict myself? Very well, I contradict myself . . ." "I find no fat sweeter than that which sticks to my own bones. . . ." forever, and still remember her black-dressed bulk, seated squat behind an English class desk, her embroidered collar, her voice powerful and high lilting Whitman's very words, and shafts of sunlight thru school windows that looked down on green grass 36 years ago.

From Teachers Make a Difference, *ed. Sue Sheridan (Houston: Harris Co. Department of Education, 1991). Reprinted by permission of Allen Ginsberg.*

FOURTH FLOOR, DAWN,
UP ALL NIGHT WRITING LETTERS

Pigeons shake their wings on the copper church roof
out my window across the street, a bird perched on the cross
surveys the city's blue-grey clouds. Larry Rivers
'll come at 10 AM and take my picture. I'm taking
your picture, pigeons. I'm writing you down, Dawn.
I'm immortalizing your exhaust, Avenue A bus.
O Thought, now you'll have to think the same thing forever!

6:48 a.m. June 7, 1980

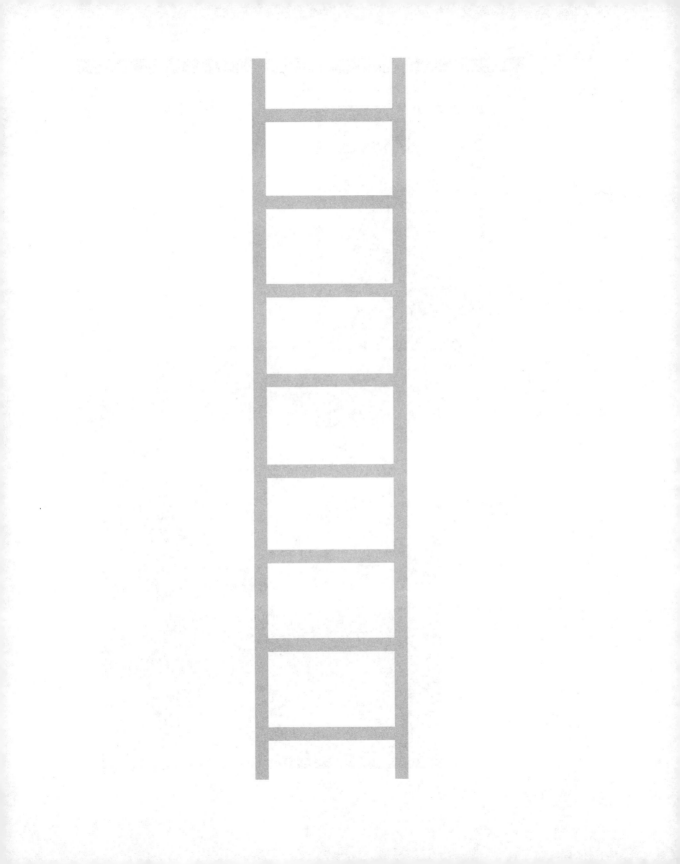

NIKKI GIOVANNI

I have always liked reading which quite naturally means I would have also enjoyed, as a young person, writing. I used to make up poems and stories for myself, draw treasure maps and dream of living on an island where I would sail the seas in search of adventure.

11

THE WORLD IS NOT A
PLEASANT PLACE TO BE

the world is not a pleasant place
to be without
someone to hold and be held by

a river would stop
its flow if only
a stream were there
to receive it

an ocean would never laugh
if clouds weren't there
to kiss her tears

the world is not
a pleasant place to be without
someone

[17 feb 72]

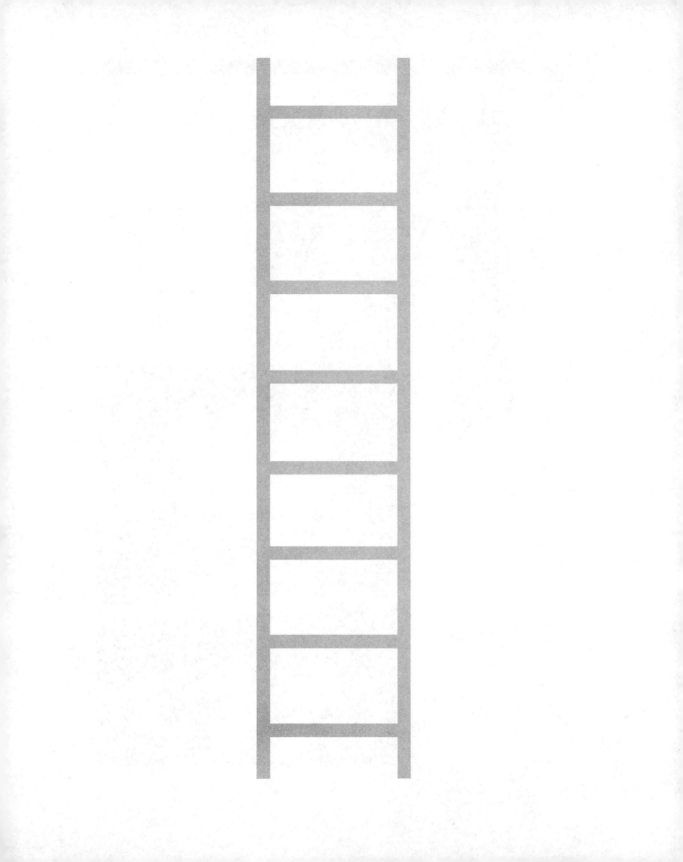

ANDREW HUDGINS

As a child, I loved to lie on my bed, turn my back to my brother, whose bed was across from mine, and slip away into the world of the book I was reading. I escaped into another world. I entered the book's life and grew both larger and smaller—larger to be living someone else's life unbeknownst to my mother and father, smaller because the book's world seemed so much larger, happier, and more exciting than mine. But when I had to stop reading and leave that other world, my own world, on my return, had grown larger too because I knew it better by comparison and contrast to the world inside the book.

But I couldn't help but notice that the books never seemed to include a child's anger, a child's rage at his own powerlessness and incomprehension, and I vowed that if I ever wrote about my own childhood I'd try to show that rage. And that's one of the things I tried to do in these poems.

CHILDHOOD OF THE ANCIENTS

Hard? You don't know what hard is, boy:
When I was your age we got up in pitch dark,
and walked five miles to school and ten miles back,
uphill both ways, and all we had for lunch
was a cold sweet potato and dry cornbread.
And when we got back home your grandma made us
chop cotton, slop the hogs, then milk the chickens
before supper, and all we had to eat
was chicken-fried pine straw and redeye gravy.
Maybe some turnip greens. Maybe some collards.
But what do you know? Shoot, you've always had
hot food plopped in front of you, like magic.
For you, it's all ice cream and soda pop.

TREE

I'd like to be a tree. My father clinked
his fork down on his plate and stared at me.
"Boy, sometimes you say the dumbest things."
You ought to know, I muttered, and got backhanded
out of my chair. Nowdays, when I chop wood
and my hands gum with resin and bark flakes,
I hunker at the tap and wash them human.
But in math class, I'd daydream of my choices:
not hickory or cedar, not an oak—
post, red, live, pin, or water oak. Just pine.
If not longleaf, I'd settle for loblolly.
My skin would thicken with harsh bark, my limbs
sprout twigs, my twigs sprout elegant green needles.
Too soon, Miz Gorrie'd call on me. "Why did
you do step four that way?" *Who me? Step four?*
"Yes, Andrew, you. Step four." *Beats me. It looked
good at the time, I guess*—and got invited
to come back after school and guess again.
And that's when I decided it: scrub pine.

THE AIR

Because I'd seen a man
thrust his straight fingers through
a melon, I spent childhood
stalking a long hall, punching
the air in front of me.
Punch where your throat would be!
Kick where your crotch would be!
the sensei yelled. I grunted,
screamed fiercely, and snapped my fists,
driving them through the soft parts
of the me that wasn't there.
I punched pure air and tried
to shatter it—the air,
which simply opened, fell back,
gave way as my hands slashed through.
The air! I can't believe
how much I hated it.

MILTON KESSLER

Poetry and childhood? A vast question. A poet is a lot like an infant. You fall and creep and stagger and reach and shake and hold. You know not one word, can tell no story, repeat no image. You are speechless. You are growing a billion cells or trillions so fast. Your cells are full of fate, angel fate or monster fate or both. The body wants to live. And speechless as the infant is it imprints itself on the world. The poet swells in the daily cave of infancy, just before words are born.

WAXWINGS

O three-toned green little place with trees,
with toy-red chimneys, one frosted, one blowing,
with tractor, toolshed, tumbling barn,
with a pink curtain in the girls' window.

O men in millhats shovel and talk,
snow so deep the cattle seem yellow.
"Out, out," the housecat flies
into the sizzling surprise.

Then waxwings snip the wick of day,
supper's good and wood is dry,
headboards hum as freight goes by.
Next morning, up and back,
every fencepost wears a cap.

GALWAY KINNELL

Childhood Music

Everything had its music and seemed to be saying something, although, because it didn't use words, I didn't always know what. The cries of roosters, at seeing daylight before anyone else, sounding like the great rusty hinges of a shed door being forced open, the hollow plod of horses' hooves on the packed dirt of Oswald Street, the sudden chinking, like some early-risen bird's, of milk bottles bumping each other as the milkman placed them on the rotting wood of the back steps, the faint, hellish, gnashing noise when my father shook down the ashes in the furnace, the impatient, rhythmical strokes of my mother scraping the burnt toast, the momentary squeak of a fingernail on a blackboard in the James C. Potter School as if a skeleton were starting to write its story, a thirsty pupil putting up her hand and asking Miss McVey in the special vocabulary and somewhat shapeless accent of Pawtucket, "May I go to the bubbla?," the wind passing through a tree giving it a moment of animation, the distant sound of a hammer striking nails on a silent afternoon, the groan of the Seekonk Lace Mill's evening whistle telling the workers they could finally go home.

Sometimes people's voices were just as wordless and mysterious. Once I walked onto the porch of the neighbors' house and through the open door saw them sitting facing each other. They seemed to be talking. I was about to knock, when I suddenly heard little whistled kiss-noises and melodies passing between them. Later my mother said that they had been sitting quietly and their canaries had been singing to one another. Sometimes, from upstairs, without being able to make out their actual words, we children could hear our parents talking, my mother's high, vigorous, impassioned, melodic sentences, such as *laleeloleedileedooleechewleemewleeboom,* punctuated by my father's deep, one-syllable reply, like a period or exclamation mark, *Hunh!*

As a child I was practically mute. I rarely spoke even when spoken to. People often asked my mother, "Has the cat got his tongue?" I still don't understand the question but even then I knew it meant people thought it odd that I was so silent.

I wanted to get my tongue back. I wanted to sing.

One day I found an old book of poetry, called *Palgrave's Golden Treasury.* In it, I discovered that there were poets who had the same thoughts as I had—thoughts I never dared tell anyone—and here they were printed in a book for all the world to see. Immediately I felt less alone and, because many of these poems seemed to speak for me, less mute. As I read, I discovered that John Keats at times wished he could leave the earth entirely and that Emily Dickinson thought of her life as a "beautiful but bleak condition." Edgar Allan Poe confessed that every night:

> I lie down by the side
> Of my darling, my darling, my life and my bride,
> In her sepulchre there by the sea—
> In her tomb by the sounding sea.

This thought made my scalp crawl but I loved it.

When they told their secret feelings, these poets were not regarded as peculiar—far from being shunned, they had become famous, *very* famous, or how could *Palgrave's Golden Treasury* have made its way into a small bookcase in a house in Pawtucket, Rhode Island?—and, years and years after being written, their poems were still being read.

When I found the world of poets, I realized I was not so odd after all. And when, one day, a teacher mentioned that Robert Frost was living and writing on a farm only a few hundred miles north of Pawtucket, I realized that poetry was not an extinct art, that poets could still exist in the world. And I started to write poetry.

BLACKBERRY EATING

I love to go out in late September
among the fat, overripe, icy, black blackberries
to eat blackberries for breakfast,
the stalks very prickly, a penalty
they earn for knowing the black art
of blackberry-making; and as I stand among them
lifting the stalks to my mouth, the ripest berries
fall almost unbidden to my tongue,
as words sometimes do, certain peculiar words
like *strengths* or *squinched,*
many-lettered, one-syllabled lumps,
which I squeeze, squinch open, and splurge well
in the silent, startled, icy, black language
of blackberry-eating in late September.

ANOTHER NIGHT IN THE RUINS

1

In the evening
haze darkening on the hills,
purple
of the eternal, a last bird
crosses over, '*flop flop,*'
adoring
only the instant.

2

Nine years ago,
in a plane that rumbled all night
above the Atlantic,
I could see, lit up
by lightning bolts jumping out of it,
a thunderhead formed like the face
of my brother, looking nostalgically down
on blue,
lightning-flashed moments of the Atlantic.

3

He used to tell me,
"What good is the day?
On some hill of despair
the bonfire
you kindle can light the great sky—

though it's true, of course, to make it burn
you have to throw yourself in . . ."

4
Wind tears itself hollow
in the eaves of my ruins, ghost-flute
of snowdrifts
that build out there in the dark:
upside-down
ravines into which night sweeps
our torn wings, our ink-spattered feathers.

5
I listen.
I hear nothing. Only
the cow, the cow
of nothingness, mooing
down the bones.

6
Is that a
rooster? He
thrashes in the snow
for a grain. Finds
it. Rips
it into
flames. Flaps. Crows.
Flames
bursting out of his brow.

7
How many nights must it take
one such as me to learn
that we aren't, after all, made
from that bird which flies out of its ashes,
that for a man
as he goes up in flames, his one work
is
to open himself, to *be*
the flames?

CAROLYN KIZER

Both my mother and my father read poetry aloud to me when I was a child. I am sure that this is one of the major reasons why I am a poet. But if I were not a poet, I would still be a lover of poetry, because of this. And we need audiences as much as we need poets! I hope your parents read aloud to you, and I also hope that when you become parents you will read to your children. Sitting in someone's lap, hearing a beloved voice speak the words and explain the hard parts, and patiently repeat a poem you've heard dozens of times—because you like it!—that's how we fall in love with words. And that's love that lasts for a lifetime.

THE GREAT BLUE HERON

M.A.K., SEPTEMBER, 1880–SEPTEMBER, 1955

As I wandered on the beach
I saw the heron standing
Sunk in the tattered wings
He wore as a hunchback's coat.
Shadow without a shadow,
Hung on invisible wires
From the top of a canvas day,
What scissors cut him out?
Superimposed on a poster
Of summer by the strand
Of a long-decayed resort,
Poised in the dusty light
Some fifteen summers ago;
I wondered, an empty child,
"Heron, whose ghost are you?"

I stood on the beach alone,
In the sudden chill of the burned.
My thought raced up the path.
Pursuing it, I ran
To my mother in the house
And led her to the scene.
The spectral bird was gone.
But her quick eye saw him drifting
Over the highest pines
On vast, unmoving wings.
Could they be those ashen things,

So grounded, unwieldy, ragged,
A pair of broken arms
That were not made for flight?
In the middle of my loss
I realized she knew:
My mother knew what he was.

O great blue heron, now
That the summer house has burned
So many rockets ago,
So many smokes and fires
And beach-lights and water-glow
Reflecting pin-wheel and flare:
The old logs hauled away,
The pines and driftwood cleared
From that bare strip of shore
Where dozens of children play;
Now there is only you
Heavy upon my eye.
Why have you followed me here,
Heavy and far away?
You have stood there patiently
For fifteen summers and snows,
Denser than my repose,
Bleaker than any dream,
Waiting upon the day
When, like gray smoke, a vapor
Floating into the sky,
A handful of paper ashes,
My mother would drift away.

TED KOOSER

When I was quite young, I was introduced to Walter de la Mare's "The Listeners," and I was so taken by it that I have been writing my own versions ever since. I can see a little of that poem in everything I've written. "Myrtle" is yet another of those passersby, stopping at a door.

MYRTLE

Wearing her yellow rubber slicker,
Myrtle, our *Journal* carrier,
has come early through rain and darkness
to bring us the news.
A woman of thirty or so,
with three small children at home,
she's told me she likes
a long walk by herself in the morning.
And with pride in her work,
she's wrapped the news neatly in plastic—
a bread bag, beaded with rain,
that reads WONDER.
From my doorway I watch her
flicker from porch to porch as she goes,
a yellow candle flame
no wind or weather dare extinguish.

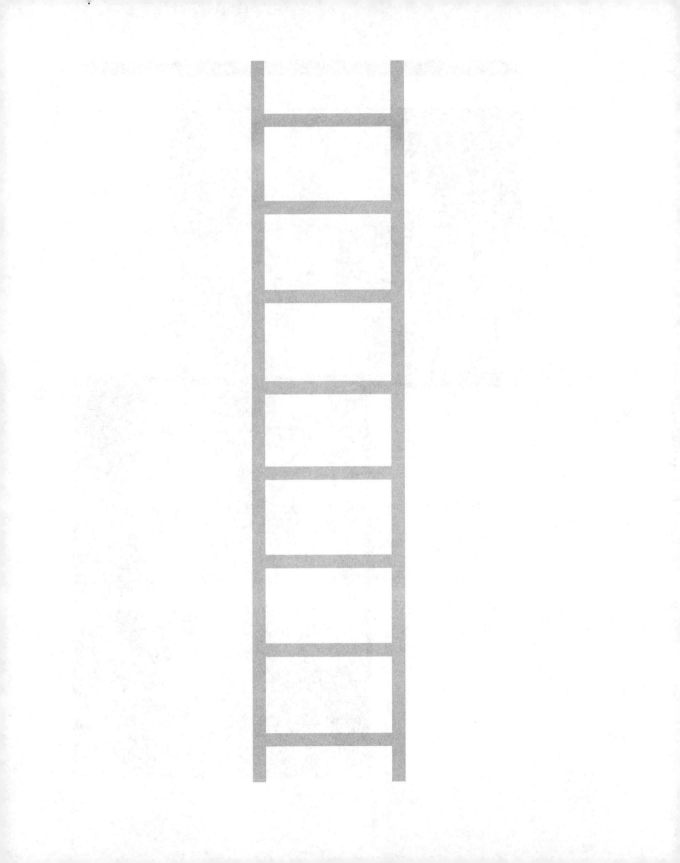

MAXINE KUMIN

I wrote my first poem when I was 8, and one of my brothers, who was good at drawing, illustrated it with a very fat robin. I never stopped reading and writing poems from that day forward but I didn't expect to become a "real" poet—my life plan was to be a famous swimmer! I also vowed to have lots of animals, especially horses, and that part of the plan has come true. I find that poetry and horses go together very well and I can't imagine living without either.

THE RETRIEVAL SYSTEM

It begins with my dog, now dead, who all his long life
carried about in his head the brown eyes of my father,
keen, loving, accepting, sorrowful, whatever;
they were Daddy's all right, handed on, except
for their phosphorescent gleam tunneling the night
which I have to concede was a separate gift.

Uncannily when I'm alone these features
come up to link my lost people
with the patient domestic beasts of my life. For example,
the wethered goat who runs free in pasture and stable
with his flecked, agate eyes and his minus-sign pupils
blats in the tiny voice of my former piano teacher

whose bones beat time in my dreams and whose terrible breath
soured "Country Gardens," "Humoresque," and unplayable Bach.
My elderly aunts, wearing the heads of willful
intelligent ponies, stand at the fence begging apples.
The sister who died at three has my cat's faint chin,
my cat's inscrutable squint, and cried catlike in pain.

I remember the funeral. *The Lord is my shepherd,*
we said. I don't want to brood. Fact: it is people who fade,
it is animals that retrieve them. A boy
I loved once keeps coming back as my yearling colt,
cocksure at the gallop, racing his shadow
for the hell of it. He runs merely to be.

A boy who was lost in the war thirty years ago
and buried at sea.

Here, it's forty degrees and raining. The weatherman
who looks like my resident owl, the one who goes out and in
by the open haymow, appears on the TV screen.
With his heart-shaped face, he is also my late dentist's double,
donnish, bifocaled, kind. Going a little gray,
advising this wisdom tooth will have to come out someday,
meanwhile filling it as a favor. Another save.
It outlasted him. The forecast is nothing but trouble.
It will snow fiercely enough to fill all these open graves.

103

STANLEY KUNITZ

In the house of my childhood and early teens in Worcester, Massachusetts, my favorite room was the library, where I would tuck myself into the faded green Morris chair, with the unabridged *Century Dictionary* on my lap, having made a pledge to learn at least one new word every day. That precious dictionary was left behind by the father I never knew, and when I touched it I felt I was touching him.

Behind our house at the edge of town stretched the dark and secret woods, whose muffled bird-songs and animal stirrings lured me in. I would race down the overgrown old trails, deep into the Indian past, shouting the words I had discovered, preferably the long ones—words like "eleemosynary" and "phantasmagoria," whose sounds excited and enchanted me. My destination was a clearing in which stood an ancient white oak, king of the wood, that dwarfed all the surrounding vegetation. In a poem of mine, "The Testing-Tree," I have described how, at fifty measured paces, I would aim three stones at my target. My fate was determined by the rules of the game I had invented. If I hit the trunk once, somebody would love me; if I hit it twice, I would be a poet; if I scored all three times, I would never die. Do I dare reveal now that I became so expert at my stone throwing that I scarcely ever missed?

Poetry, I have come to believe, is ultimately mythology, the telling of the stories of the soul in its journey through this life, its passage through time and history.

THE PORTRAIT

My mother never forgave my father
for killing himself,
especially at such an awkward time
and in a public park,
that spring
when I was waiting to be born.
She locked his name
in her deepest cabinet
and would not let him out,
though I could hear him thumping.
When I came down from the attic
with the pastel portrait in my hand
of a long lipped stranger
with a brave moustache
and deep brown level eyes,
she ripped it into shreds
without a single word
and slapped me hard.
In my sixty-fourth year
I can feel my cheek
still burning.

AFTER THE LAST DYNASTY

Reading in Li Po
how "the peach blossom follows the water"
I keep thinking of you
because you were so much like
Chairman Mao,
naturally with the sex
transposed
and the figure slighter.
Loving you was a kind
of Chinese guerrilla war.
Thanks to your lightfoot genius
no Eighth Route Army
kept its lines more fluid,
traveled with less baggage,
so nibbled the advantage.
Even with your small bad heart
you made a dance of departures.
In the cold spring rains
when last you failed me
I had nothing left to spend
but a red crayon language
on the character of the enemy
to break appointments,
to fight us not
with his strength
but with his weakness,

to kill us
not with his health
but with his sickness.

Pet, spitfire, blue-eyed pony,
here is a new note
I want to pin on your door,
though I am ten years late
and you are nowhere:
Tell me,
are you still mistress of the valley,
what trophies drift downriver,
why did you keep me waiting?

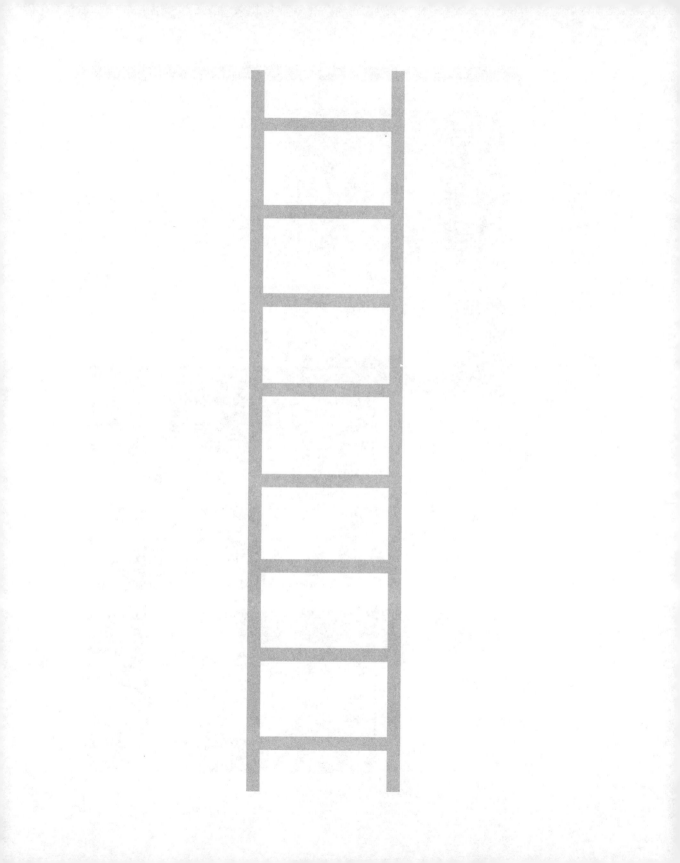

GREG KUZMA

When I write for children I am writing for myself. I have not lost my sense of the magic and wonder of the world. My earliest experiences with books were nursery rhymes, where I hardly knew half of what was being read me by my kindly Grandma Bradshaw. Much of the new work I am doing reclaims these moments, where word and thing meet and kiss, the world of language and the world of objects and events are joined in an affectionate embrace.

The poet is the child alive in the greater world, bearing the magic book of words. I am this same child I was, the world around me a constant dazzle and mystery. Each day is a new birth, each night comes down like the final night. The child's world is mine.

NIGHT THINGS

The wind has all its answers
in a sock.
The rock has a book it says
and reads it every night.
It's called the river.
Mouse with gray eyes, feet
like broken toothpicks,
runs when the moon comes up.

ICE SKATING

Ten rains, and then snow, then more snow, then
a very cold period, then snow again, then the snow
went away, but the ground seemed frozen still,
the lake ice got better, we started skating again,
then a big snow came, the ice got covered,
and we had to go up and shovel.
Everywhere we wanted to skate, to put our thin blades down
we had to shovel.
It was like starting fresh on the earth,
the whole earth thinking of something else,
bent on evolving some entirely other form of life,
when out of the tenuous small houses
they had built for themselves, and were hanging on in,
just this side of sanity and survival,
the strange creatures came,
wrapped in rags, the big one
carrying an armload of sticks,
the littler ones following,
and then the scraping noises,
followed by grunts, followed by oohs and ahs,
silence,
and a skimming sound, like wind through branches.

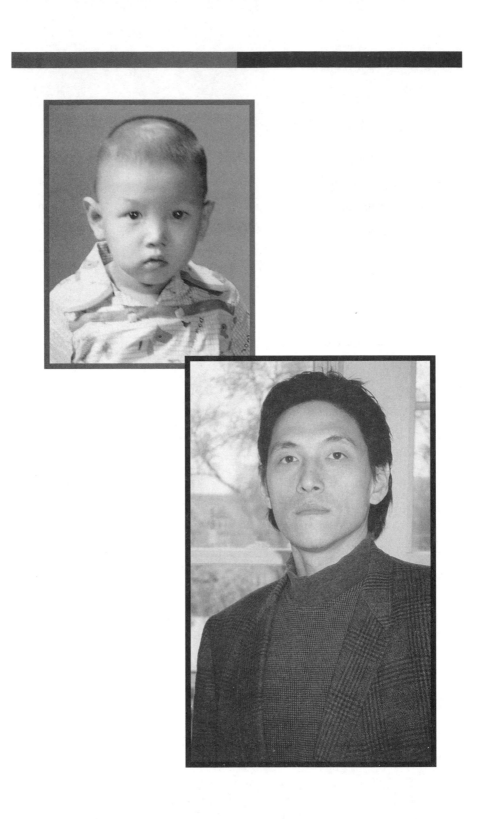

LI-YOUNG LEE

I knew as a child that no one knew me, that, even given the names adults gave me, I remained a secret to them and to myself. Poetry safeguards or is that place at which we stand unknown to ourselves, yet fully revealed. So it seems to me.

EATING TOGETHER

In the steamer is the trout
seasoned with slivers of ginger,
two sprigs of green onion, and sesame oil.
We shall eat it with rice for lunch,
brothers, sister, my mother who will
taste the sweetest meat of the head,
holding it between her fingers
deftly, the way my father did
weeks ago. Then he lay down
to sleep like a snow-covered road
winding through pines older than him,
without any travelers, and lonely for no one.

I ASK MY MOTHER TO SING

She begins, and my grandmother joins her.
Mother and daughter sing like young girls.
If my father were alive, he would play
his accordion and sway like a boat.

I've never been in Peking, or the Summer Palace,
nor stood on the great Stone Boat to watch
the rain begin on Kuen Ming Lake, the picnickers
running away in the grass.

But I love to hear it sung;
how the waterlilies fill with rain until
they overturn, spilling water into water,
then rock back, and fill with more.

Both women have begun to cry.
But neither stops her song.

HEATHER McHUGH

O ne of the Zen Fathers, who are always offering mysterious advice, was said to have recommended: "In order to write haiku, get a three-foot child." Some days I think he meant the child to be the writer, some days I think the model. In any case, I believe a good half of the work of writing is the work of recovering (maybe discovering is closer to the light) a fresh mind. That's why I love MacLuhan's story (true) of the kid taken for his first airplane ride, remaining silent while strapped in, silent during taxi and take-off, silent until cruising altitude—when he turned to his father and asked, "When do we start getting smaller?" Never of course; and also soon.

A NIGHT IN A WORLD

I wouldn't have known if I didn't stay home
where the big dipper rises from, time
and again: one mountain ash.

And I wouldn't have thought without travelling out
how huge that dipper was,
how small that tree.

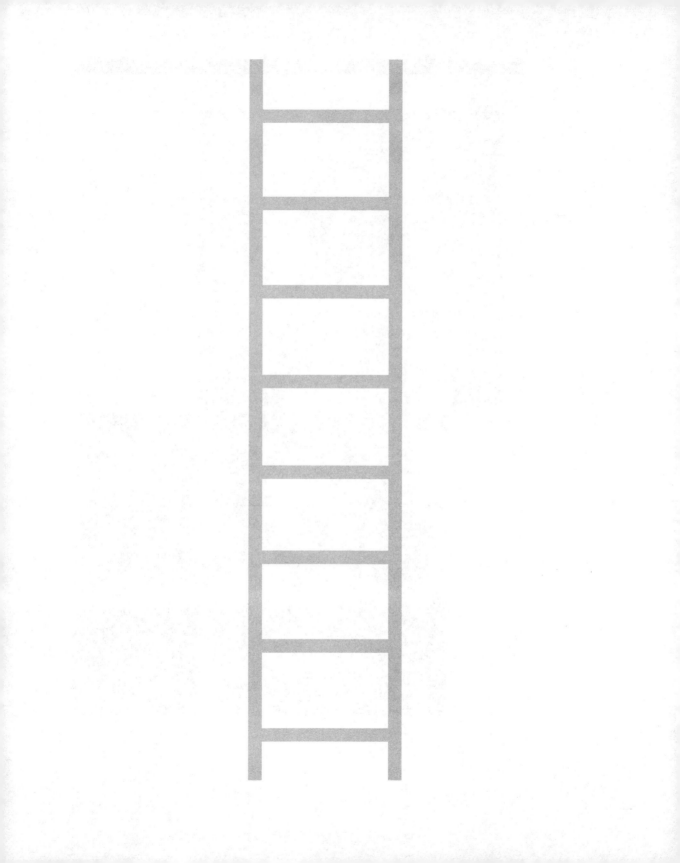

KYOKO MORI

For me, poems are about unexpected connections. When I start working on a poem, I often have a handful of images that seem to bring together the past and the present. I work with these images and the stories that they call forth—until I know what the connections are, precisely. What I find out is almost always slightly different from what I thought I would find out—the poem ends up just a short distance away from where I thought it was going at first (not a great distance: if it were an actual distance, it would be a block or two away, sometimes even just kitty-corner).

In this process of finding the connections, I am almost always writing about my childhood. The images from childhood are unforgettable: the flowers in my mother's garden, my favorite black velvet dress, the day my brother tried to cut off his eyelashes because they were long and beautiful and everyone told him he was pretty enough to be a girl. . . . In a way, such images and memories are points of reference. I have a poor sense of direction. Sometimes, facing north, I can't remember if east is to my right or to my left. In those moments of confusion, I picture myself in my bedroom in Ashiya, Japan, where my mother taught me about the four directions: the verandah is to the south, the piano is the east, the door to the kitchen is the west, my mother's embroidered wall-hanging is tacked on the north wall. In poems and in life, childhood memories point the way—they keep me from getting lost.

BARBIE SAYS MATH IS HARD

As a boy, I'd still have asked
why Jack must spend exactly
two dollars at the corner store.
Give him a coin purse is as
good an answer as five apples
and two oranges. Also: would
he bake the apples into pies
or cobblers, save the orange peel
in glass jars to spice up his
tea or cake? If his father
paints their house with Mr. Jones,
which man will take the peaks and
why? Would the raspberry beetles
swarm over wet paint? Why is
Mr. Jones slower than his
neighbor? If x equals y,
is it like putting apples into
cole slaw, the way a tomato
is really a fruit? None of my
dolls talked or grew hair. In
third grade, Satsuki and I
traded our Barbies' limbs so
mine could flex her left biceps
while hers sat cross-legged
raising one stiff arm
like a weapon. If Satsuki has
daughters, she might remember

the grasshoppers we caught,
how we cupped two hands together
into crooked globes to
hear them rattling inside like
a small motor. She would tell
her daughters: Yes, math was hard,
but not because we were girls.

SHARON OLDS

From when I was a newborn, I heard every Sunday a distinctive four-beat rhythm—ONE and TWO and THREE and FOUR (or, *and ONE and TWO and THREE and FOUR*)—a set of four strong and four weak accents that occurred, itself, in sets of four:

> ONWard CHRISTian SO-OLDIERS
> MARChing OFF TO-O WA-a-AR
> WITH the CROSS of JE-SUS
> GOing ON beFO-ORE.

This was the art form I heard. Luckily it was not the only one. I heard the *Psalms* from the Old Testament—and I heard birds, and wind in trees, and lake water, and the ocean at the beach. And I saw flowers (I liked to look at them up very close), and sky, and clouds, and people. There were many different patterns stored in me. But when I started to write poems, what came out were four-beat lines in four-line stanzas (quatrains), the form I was imprinted with early. That seems still to be the underlying rhythm of what I write.

> When I *got* to the *air*port I *rushed up* to the *desk,*
> *bought* my *tick*et, *ten* minutes *lat*er
> they *told* me the *flight* was *can*celled. The *doc*tors

had *said* my *father* would *not live* through the *night*
and the *flight* was *can*celled. A *young man*

I don't try to do this, it just happens. Each poet has a different voice, from out of a different life. This is one way poetry is continually renewed.

THE RACE

When I got to the airport I rushed up to the desk,
bought a ticket, ten minutes later
they told me the flight was cancelled, the doctors
had said my father would not live through the night
and the flight was cancelled. A young man
with a dark brown moustache told me
another airline had a non-stop
leaving in seven minutes. See that
elevator over there, well go
down to the first floor, make a right, you'll
see a yellow bus, get off at the
second Pan Am terminal, I
ran, I who have no sense of direction
raced exactly where he'd told me, a fish
slipping upstream deftly against
the flow of the river. I jumped off that bus with those
bags I had thrown everything into
in five minutes, and ran, the bags
wagged me from side to side as if
to prove I was under the claims of the material,
I ran up to a man with a white flower on his breast,
I who always go to the end of the line, I said
Help me. He looked at my ticket, he said
Make a left and then a right, go up the moving stairs and then
run. I lumbered up the moving stairs,
at the top I saw the corridor,
and then I took a deep breath, I said

Goodbye to my body, goodbye to comfort,
I used my legs and heart as if I would
gladly use them up for this,
to touch him again in this life. I ran, and the
bags banged against me, wheeled and coursed
in skewed orbits, I have seen pictures of
women running, their belongings tied
in scarves grasped in their fists, I blessed my
long legs he gave me, my strong
heart I abandoned to its own purpose,

I ran to Gate 17 and they were
just lifting the thick white
lozenge of the door to fit it into
the socket of the plane. Like the one who is not
too rich, I turned sideways and
slipped through the needle's eye, and then
I walked down the aisle toward my father. The jet
was full, and people's hair was shining, they were
smiling, the interior of the plane was filled with a
mist of gold endorphin light,
I wept as people weep when they enter heaven,
in massive relief. We lifted up
gently from one tip of the continent
and did not stop until we set down lightly on the
other edge. I walked into his room
and watched his chest rise slowly
and sink again, all night
I watched him breathe.

LINDA PASTAN

In what I think of as my lonely childhood (I had no brothers or sisters), poetry kept me company. I read poems as if they were letters written to me, and I wrote poems back as answers. In a way I've been doing the same thing ever since.

EGG

In this kingdom
the sun never sets;
under the pale oval
of the sky
there seems no way in
or out,
and though there is a sea here
there is no tide.

For the egg itself
is a moon
glowing faintly
in the galaxy of the barn,
safe but for the spoon's
ominous thunder,
the first delicate crack
of lightning.

SEPTEMBER

it rained in my sleep
and in the morning the fields were wet

I dreamed of artillery
of the thunder of horses

in the morning the fields were strewn
with twigs and leaves

as if after a battle
or a sudden journey

I went to sleep in summer
I dreamed of rain

in the morning the fields were wet
and it was autumn

135

DIANA RIVERA

If one sees the world with the spirit of a child, purity of heart, and love, one is lucky. When one lives with hope and faith, one is lucky. When one attempts to re-create this world, the speech of our souls, one can be called a poet. Whether poetry is written for children or adults, poetry contains childlike qualities, the innocence of seeing, imaginative play, singleness of expression. A child's heart, an uncontaminated soul, is there. Whether poetry is written for children or adults, soul freedom, honesty, and creative spontaneity—the poet's true child-self—determine great poetry.

To be a poet is to let angels sing, to hold the innocent child with care. For truly, children are our best poets. Innocence, our best teacher.

UNDER THE APPLE TREE

I like it here,
under the apple tree,
knotty, with its hollow
belly

here
sitting on its branch
above stone fences that separate pastures,

taking life
here
with the sun that strokes the sides of trees
casting its shadows on emerald hills.

I like it here,
entering the dark crevice of trunks,
studying the butterfly's tiny blue hearts
on powdery wings.

Like horses with their swerved necks,
I concentrate on grass.
Earthworms insert themselves into the earth
like glossy, pink pins!

Against the green, a yellow shrub
furiously sprouts
in a trance of burning stars.

Branches are suns
that glimmer from within
taking life

here, under the apple tree,
where a crowd of petals close their eyes,
where scraggly layers of trunk
seem to slowly come apart.

At sunset the branch I sit on snaps and coils.
The blue jay hastily darts, and disappears.
I like it
here

where birds now nestle and sleep,
where little, high-pitched, cricketed chirps
rise like tiny bells towards the ageless moon.

Here,
where insects,—silver specks—
fly through the glimmering blue.

Oh, but the mouse hides under the hay and the cracks.
The horses trod down the pasture, disappearing
like an impression of veils.

They say this apple tree is very old,
oh, but I like it here,
sitting on its rugged branch

above stone fences that separate
dark, sleepy pastures.

DINNER TOGETHER

Sitting by the barbecue
waiting for sausages and hot dogs
blue-gray smoke the same color
of the sky
I see a tiny spider
walking down from the sky with tiny six-
footed steps
down
down
in a perfectly straight
line
all the way
down
to the floor
then back up
the same line
rising from one cloud
up to another,
a silver speck
glistening
at its mouth,
climbing the invisible ladder.

LIZ ROSENBERG

I suppose I was eight or nine when I began writing poems. My first poem, I remember, was intended to be about a pomegranate—how it looked like a nest of garnets shining inside the rind of the fruit. But "pomegranate" didn't rhyme with anything—in those days I rhymed everything—so I put in diamonds, emeralds, amethysts, pearls, everything but garnets. It was a lesson in how poems don't always say what we mean, though we try. I know I am still trying not to be so entranced or frightened by the words that I end up saying something I don't mean. I have often thought that if only I could have spoken—spoken clearly, I mean, and with confidence that I could be heard—I would never have had to write.

For my tenth birthday, a friend's mother gave me a copy of Robert Frost's book of poems *You Come Too*. I still have it, and am happy to say that book is still in print. I loved the old-fashioned way Frost used language, "I shan't be gone long, you come, too." It seemed other-worldly and magical and a place one wanted to get to. Poetry is still an escape for me—but whether into or out of something, is not yet decided.

WHICH ONE IS THE GROWN-UP? HAIKU

Oh God, God!—Calm down,
says my son, looking at me,
holding my big hand.

NO BOUNDARIES

144

For instance, the child skipping—
is not touching the earth at all, is not obeying
the laws of locomotion in any part of the body;
the hair flips in a tidal wave; the eyeballs bounce;
lips quiver; the skirt darts butterfly-like above the knees
—and part of it is the blue sky, always, open
like a palm. The child, skipping,
holds hands a moment with her own happiness.

THEY ARE PLANNING TO CANCEL THE SCHOOL MILK PROGRAM TO FUND A TAX CUT FOR THE MIDDLE CLASS

So the milk carton which used to wobble
on the little metal desk will no longer arrive,
and the child will drink instead from the school water fountain
and have a little less
each day a little less—
but now there will be more empty space, more room
in her rumpled paper bag!
and more room on the school desk
which is clamped with metal rivets to her chair.
And the middle-class man will wash his car
more often, the middle-class woman wash her hair
at a stylist's, like a decent person,
and the child at the desk with one square
carton missing may find room to think thoughts
that will bring the stars, the clouds, the trees
around our heads!

145

DAVID ST. JOHN

Childhood is the time when the world first makes itself present to us. For some young future artists, the things and places and people of the world make themselves known as colors and shapes and movements; these artists may become painters and the makers of movies. Some future artists sense the world as melody, rhythm and song; these young people may become musicians. But for some of us, the world of our childhood finds its presence most powerfully in *language,* in the voices of other people and the beauty and power of words themselves. Of course, for a writer, words also carry with them the shapes and colors of the visual arts, as well as the rhythms and melody of music.

The magic of poetry is that, as a writer, one can begin to re-create the world one experiences in all of its power; one can try to give the reader him- or herself that experience of the world *in language* and *as language.* In poems we experience our world through the visions and voices of other people who share that world with us. In that way, our own experiences and our own lives become richer and more pleasing. All art—painting, music, and poetry—help us to understand the passions and beauties and dilemmas of our lives, and art helps us to enjoy and make sense of our world. To be an artist of any kind, I believe, is the noblest accomplishment one can ever hope to achieve.

GUITAR

I have always loved the word *guitar.*

I have no memories of my father on the patio
At dusk, strumming a Spanish tune,
Or my mother draped in that fawn wicker chair
Polishing her flute;
I have no memories of your song, distant Sister
Heart, of those steel strings sliding
All night through the speaker of the car radio
Between Tucumcari and Oklahoma City, Oklahoma.
Though I've never believed those stories
Of gypsy cascades, stolen horses, castanets,
And stars, of Airstream trailers and good fortune,
Though I never met Charlie Christian, though
I've danced the floors of cold longshoremen's halls,
Though I've waited with the overcoats at the rear
Of concerts for lute, mandolin, and two guitars—
More than the music I love scaling its woven
Stairways, more than the swirling chocolate of wood

I have always loved the word *guitar.*

MAURYA SIMON

I wrote my first poem when I was seven and living in Paris with my family. One day, while my mother, sister, and I were walking out of the city's huge park, the Bois de Boulougne, we happened upon a fantastic, royal wedding procession. Here's the poem:

> Once when I lived in Paris,
> I stopped to see a carriage
> carrying lovers to a marriage
> in the church of Acolox.
> And a man with a ring in a box,
> and a bride with golden hair
> were tossing flowers everywhere.

This poem reminds me of where poetry started for me: in my ears and eyes—that is, the world seemed and *still* seems like a wonderful carnival to feast upon. So, poems for me are a kind of marriage between images and the rattle, click, or rustling of the right words moving against each other in the eye, ear, and mind.

NIGHT

Now, as the stars unfleece themselves,
the moon in its chalky house
lights its translucent fire and swells.
All the feathered songs are quiet,
all the rustlings of the day fold up
their sounds and settle into silence.

STANDING BETWEEN TWO IDEAS

You might have been a meadowlark making
your way over winter's blue fields, or I,
a mole awakening to a feast of fennel.
There's no way of knowing if this life
is the one fate promised to us.

But we've been fitted to stand upright:
to speak, to weep, to have faith in a god.
And whether we soar or simply shuffle
our feet, seems also a matter of fate.
Circumstances aren't purely accidental.

I sometimes think destiny can be outwitted,
that we can shake off these tame skins
and step into the sinews of another being—
that we can arch our backs and leap,
and hoof our way up to heaven.

W. D. SNODGRASS

Poetry gives us the chance, for a brief while, to try on someone else's thoughts and so to move—and perhaps develop—part of the mind's musculature which would go sloppy with disuse. So doing, it gives us more chance to choose, to decide about who we shall become. Not that this is easy, but most of the things we really enjoy aren't, either. Like basketball or riddles, poetry is one of the things we'd call hard work, if they weren't so much fun.

FROM SNOW SONGS

i.
one. now another. one
more. some again; then done.
though others run
down your windshield, when
up ahead a sudden
swirl and squall comes on
like moths, mayflies in a swarm
against your lights, a storm
of small fry, seeds, unknown
species, populations. every one
particular and special; each one
melting, breaking, hurling on
into the blank black. soon,
never to be seen again.
most never seen.
all, gone.

156

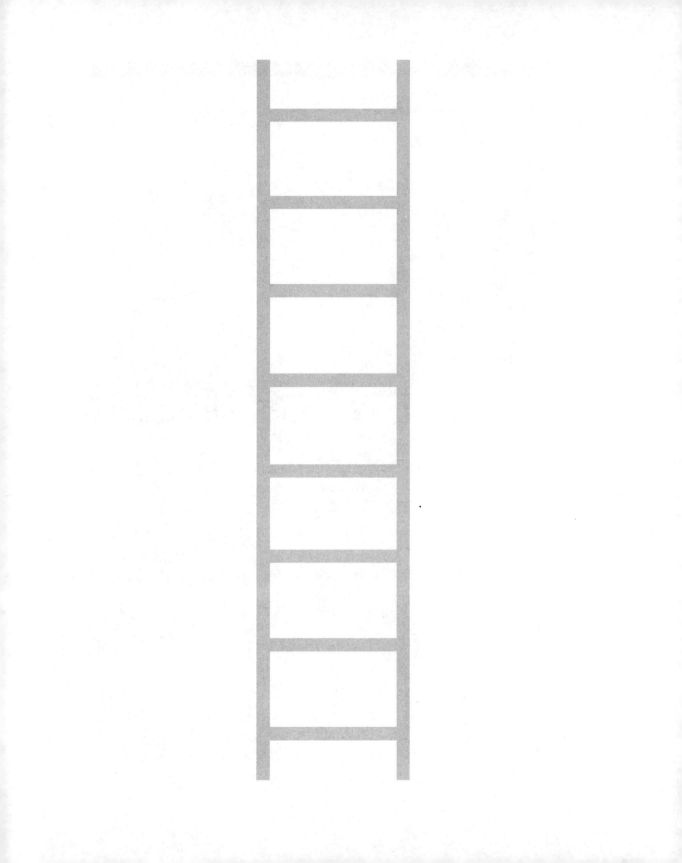

GERALD STERN

Of the many things a poet has, one of them is the ability to be childlike, that is, to be clear-sighted, open, available, eager, and ready. These things are expressed through attitude, and attitude is expressed in language, as far as poets are concerned. Children should listen to poets; poets should listen to them!

159

ROYAL MANOR ROAD

It would be worth it to go ninety miles out of your way
to see these cows eat and sleep and nuzzle in the mud.
It would be worth it to leave the tables at Grand Ticino
and walk down Thompson Street talking about the eyes—
"Are they the eyes of Kora, are they soft and slanted;
are they the eyes of Juno and drunken Hathor?"
All my reading, all my difficult reading
would be worth it as I stood in the weeds
watching them run up like kittens, watching them
crowd each other for little tastes of clover and hepatica.
To reach my hand inside
and touch the bony forehead and the stiff hair
would be worth it.

BEHAVING LIKE A JEW

When I got there the dead opossum looked like
an enormous baby sleeping on the road.
It took me only a few seconds—just
seeing him there—with the hole in his back
and the wind blowing through his hair
to get back again into my animal sorrow.
I am sick of the country, the bloodstained
bumpers, the stiff hairs sticking out of the grilles,
the slimy highways, the heavy birds
refusing to move;
I am sick of the spirit of Lindbergh over everything,
that joy in death, that philosophical
understanding of carnage, that
concentration on the species.
—I am going to be unappeased at the opossum's death.
I am going to behave like a Jew
and touch his face, and stare into his eyes,
and pull him off the road.
I am not going to stand in a wet ditch
with the Toyotas and the Chevies passing over me
at sixty miles an hour
and praise the beauty and the balance
and lose myself in the immortal lifestream
when my hands are still a little shaky
from his stiffness and his bulk
and my eyes are still weak and misty
from his round belly and his curved fingers
and his black whiskers and his little dancing feet.

FROM LUCKY LIFE

Dear waves, what will you do for me this year?
Will you drown out my scream?
Will you let me rise through the fog?
Will you fill me with that old salt feeling?
Will you let me take my long steps in the cold sand?
Will you let me lie on the white bedspread and study
the black clouds with the blue holes in them?
Will you let me see the rusty trees and the old monoplanes one more
    year?
Will you still let me draw my sacred figures
and move the kites and the birds around with my dark mind?

Lucky life is like this. Lucky there is an ocean to come to.
Lucky you can judge yourself in this water.
Lucky the waves are cold enough to wash out the meanness.
Lucky you can be purified over and over again.
Lucky there is the same cleanliness for everyone.
Lucky life is like that. Lucky life. Oh lucky life.
Oh lucky lucky life. Lucky life.

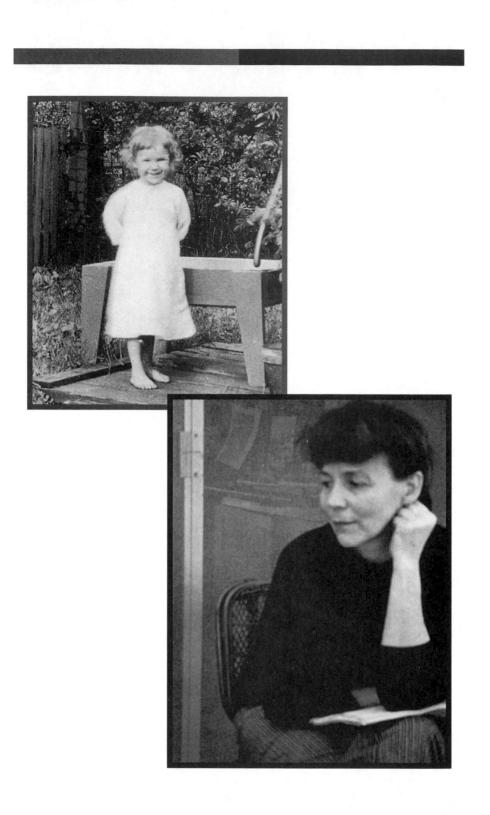

RUTH STONE

I remember my mother reading poems to me and she told me later that she read those poems out loud when I was a baby. I think the rhythm of those poems stayed always in my head. And then my father played drums and when he practiced at home those rhythms stayed with me. And the sounds of words were like music. I believe all children are born into music and poetry. It is the natural beat of the heart and the natural way of the mind with language. It is how we are. The way color and form and sound all come together in the arts and are natural to us from the beginning. These are the important things that children know. These are the paths into knowing and experiencing the world and ourselves in the world. These are the ways we speak to one another from our deepest selves.

THE NOSE

Everyone complains about the nose.
If you notice, it is stuck to your face.
In the morning it will be red.
If you are a woman you can cover it with makeup.
If you are a man it means you had a good time last night.
Noses are phallic symbols.
So are fingers, monuments, trees, and cucumbers.
The familiar, "He knows his stuff," should be looked into.
There is big business in nose jobs,
The small nose having gained popularity during the Christian boom.
Noses get out of joint but a broken nose
Is never the same thing as a broken heart.
They say, "Bless your heart." "Shake hands." "Blow
    your nose."
When kissing there is apt to be a battle of wills
Over which side your nose will go on.
While a nosebleed, next to a good cry, is a natural physic;
A nosey person smells you out and looking down your nose
Will make you cross-eyed.
Although the nose is no longer used for rooting and shoving,
It still gets into some unlikely places.
The old sayings: He won by a nose, and,
He cut off his nose to spite his face,
Illustrate the value of the nose.
In conclusion, three out of four children
Are still equipped with noses at birth;
And the nose, more often than not,
Accompanies the body to its last resting place.

LUCIEN STRYK

What can I say about poetry? Since I was a very young lad, whether glad, mad, or frustrated, I always found that writing a poem made me feel better about the day. I remember racing home from school, eager to get out to play, only to be told to baby-sit my sister and get my homework done while my mother shopped. First I sulked and pouted, feeling really hard done by, moped about the apartment, envying my friends. Finally, I flopped down on the red rug, pen and notebook in hand to do my homework. Instead of getting into math, which I most hated, I began to doodle, and my doodle turned into a jingle—the jingle my first poem, "On a Red Rug."

DAWN

Five a.m., and I've been
up for hours. My lamp,
false star, holds back

the dark. In the next
room my wife guards our
closeness deep in dream.

I love this sleeplessness,
cloistered unbroken
hours over a spotless page,

the book with all the
answers on the shelf. I
doodle on one, thumb

through the other, now
and then. This hour, it
makes no difference.

I sit back, let thoughts
come as they may. Who
knows, before dawn rides

the oak across the way,
the book may jostle just a
bit, the paper bear a poem.

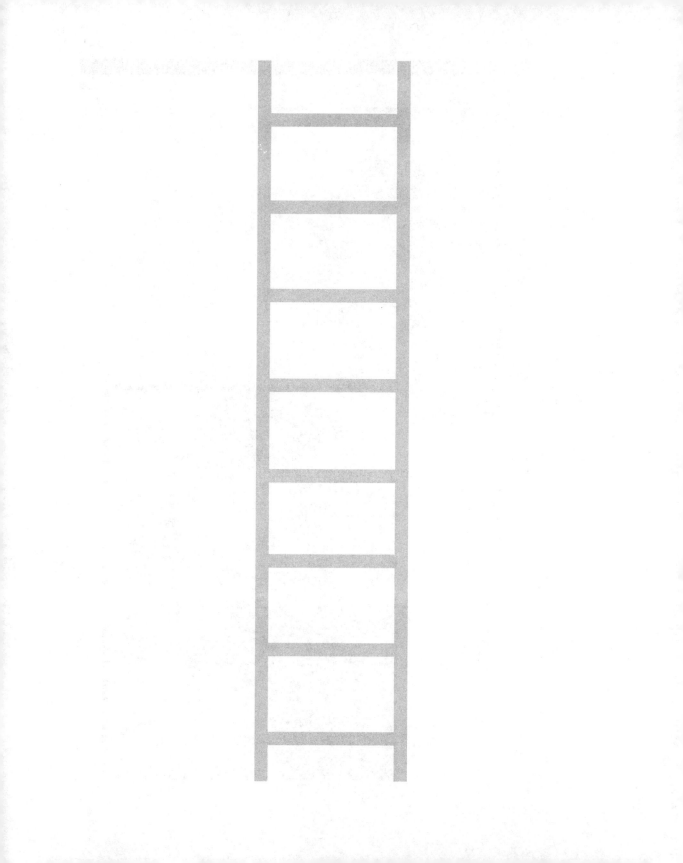

ALICE WALKER

Poetry breaks through the skin of suffering in which children are often imprisoned: silent, confused, scared. A child's poetry is an intimate, trusting gift to her parent or to anyone who wishes to "read" her heart.

173

REMEMBER?

Remember me?
I am the girl
with the dark skin
whose shoes are thin
I am the girl
with rotted teeth
I am the dark
rotten-toothed girl
with the wounded eye
and the melted ear.

I am the girl
holding their babies
cooking their meals
sweeping their yards
washing their clothes
Dark and rotting
and wounded, wounded.

I would give
to the human race
only hope.

I am the woman
with the blessed
dark skin
I am the woman
with teeth repaired
I am the woman
with the healing eye
the ear that hears.

I am the woman: Dark,
repaired, healed
Listening to you.

I would give
to the human race
only hope.

I am the woman
offering two flowers
whose roots
are twin

Justice and Hope

Let us begin.

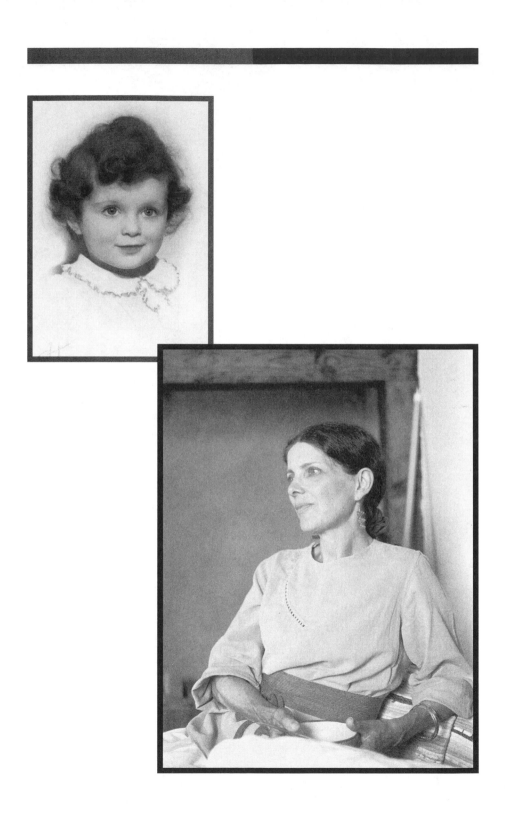

JANE O. WAYNE

In some mysterious way, a poem often works the way a joke does. You get it or you don't. And right away. Of course, a reader should go back, again and again, for ideas, for hidden meanings, for special wording, or maybe simply for the pleasure itself, but the strange magic of poetry—its music, beauty, mood—some of that should strike you right away.

Although a careful reader will take a poem apart to learn how it works, the way a mechanic might a car, I like to think that when a poem succeeds, you usually know it on impact. But unlike a joke, if a poem is truly good, the more you read it, the better it gets.

BY ACCIDENT

Because I brought him here
I hold his hand
while the surgeon cleans his leg,
a boy I hardly know, a child
my daughter's age. Years ago
a black nurse held
my white hand in a hospital and I
squeezed then just as he does now
a stranger never thanked
never forgotten.

I know how it happens,
how pain softens us as easily
as habit hardens, how
we meet now and if we meet again
we both avert our eyes,
the boy and I,
as from the gash itself,
the white seams gaping on the raw red,
we turn away. Often I think we can,
given half a chance, love anyone.

THE EAVESDROPPER

That small girl crouched
on the top steps to listen
is still waiting to hear her name
on their lips, to come alive
like a deck of cards
shuffled in their downstairs hands.

She's still motionless
outside the living room, straining
to catch some hint
that no one drops, still in that hallway
dwelling on their talk
as a thumb does a rough fingernail.

C L E A N I N G   I N D I A N   D A H L

If you watch me
picking stones out of these red lentils
pushing the tiny peas, grain by grain
across a white platter
you'll find it tedious

unless you know
that it takes more for someone else
to put them in, than for me to take them out,
that each rock was chosen carefully
by size, by color

and that the way a butcher
might rest his thumb on a scale
some man or woman, maybe even a child
boosted a poor yield
with this grit in my palm.

IN PRAISE OF ZIGZAGS

For a Girl Failing Geometry

Maybe she does her homework
the way she does her chores.
She moves quickly when she vacuums,
forgetting corners in the living room,
repeating others,
zigzags recklessly across the carpet,
raising those pale tracks
behind her in the wool, crossing
and recrossing them. And not once
does geometry cross her mind.
Outside she wanders aimlessly
behind the lawnmower,
rolls toward the middle of the lawn,
then doubles back.
For a while, she'll follow straight lines—
the fence, the hedge, the walk—
then go off on a tangent, spiraling
around the birch or the maple.
When she finishes,
she leaves the lawnmower out, leaves
a trail of unmown strips and crisscrosses,
her scribbling on the lawn
like a line of thought that's hard to follow.
As far as she's concerned
the shortest distance between two points
is confining.

DIETER WESLOWSKI

I can now say, with certainty, that the poet does not choose poetry, but the other way around. The poet is chosen because of his or her affinity (literally, from the getgo) for language, for the love of words and for playing with words. There is something magical about language—it doesn't only describe the world, but creates one.

DRY WORLD

When the sun shuts down her cantina,
the lizard goes underground,
as does the scorpion
who carries his needle of clear poison
like a lantern above his body.

ZOE AND THE GHOSTS

That evening,
after Scotty and his mother moved out,
you and I climbed steps
to the third floor balcony, watched
lightning touch down, explode
with a crack. We heard wind
rush voices
through those emptied rooms.
You asked about ghosts;
"Are there such things, Pa?" Holding
your hand, I touched fear, barely
sensing my own: those branches
of the tulip tree, thrashing back and forth,
a swimmer going under.

HEART

my old druid, winter
is here, and I have brought
love
into my house: a hawthorn
branch with long,
long thorns
and apples
so small
one could almost miss
the light
of their red lanterns.

185

PABLO,

I too am waiting
for the sea
to wash a door ashore,
the one that will be
my writing desk.

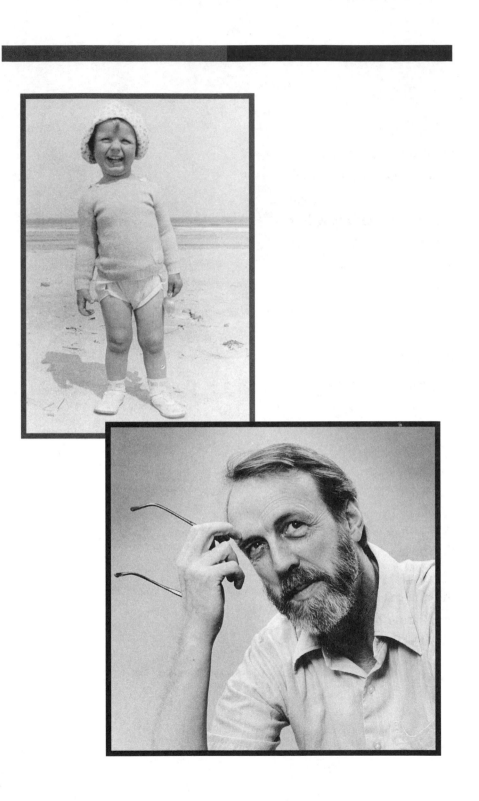

ROBLEY WILSON

Poetry seems to me a vital part of childhood, beginning with pat-a-cake and proceeding through the poems taught in schools. It's sad that poetry hasn't a larger place in public education—it peters out at about third grade, I suppose because the teachers feel they lack competence (and often they do)—because I think there's a *need* for it that we're born with. I'll always be grateful to my mother for being an amateur poet and introducing me to *A Child's Garden of Verses* when I was very young indeed. The early learning stays and shapes and rewards us all.

ENVOI

Sun in the mouth of the day.
Moon in the teeth of night—
Taste everything, they say;
Swallow nothing but light.

I WISH IN THE CITY OF YOUR HEART

I wish in the city of your heart
you would let me be the street
where you walk when you are most
yourself. I imagine the houses:
It has been raining, but the rain
is done and the children kept home
have begun opening their doors.

189

WAYS TO USE THIS BOOK

The first poem I chose for this book—Robley Wilson's "I Wish in the City of Your Heart"—turned out to be the very last poem *in* the book. That was a simple accident of the alphabet. I organized the poems by the first letter of the poet's last name and Wilson came last. Within each poet's own group of poems, I tried to put the ones for younger readers first, and for older readers last. Sometimes it was hard to tell which was which. Shorter is not always easier. A seemingly simple poem can have as many echoes in it as a voice shouted in a cavern. Some readers, of course, will read the book from beginning to end, like a novel. Others will skip around. Some might look at all the pictures of the poets first. Or read their statements and then turn to see what kind of poetry these people write.

There is no wrong way to use this book.

All the same, I have been teaching poetry for almost twenty years, so of course I have a few suggestions.

The poet Galway Kinnell says we should always learn a poem "by heart, by hand, and by mouth." That means that if you really want to get to know a poem, you'll want to memorize it, write it down in your own handwriting, and say it out loud in your own voice. This is true whether the poem is written by you or by somebody else. If I could give one piece of advice to the teachers of young poets, it would be this: ask your students to memorize two poems a month, one poem that they have written, and one written by someone else. At the end of one year they would have twenty-four poems "by heart and by mouth." That is a lot of company to have, on walks, in hospital waiting rooms, on lonely nights. Memorization and recitation fell out of favor many years ago, and some people associate it with terrible flowery poems, and humiliating moments in front of other people. It doesn't have to be like that. Young people ought to be free to choose the poems they like. Simply keeping books of poetry around, and having the chance to look through them frequently, is one way of being more comfortable with poetry. Then, too, it doesn't really matter if you keep the poem in front of you when you recite it—the point is not whether you have memorized it perfectly, but to speak the poem from the heart and mouth, as best you can. It's not a test, but an exercise of affection and respect.

There is not one single poem in this book that could not trigger an "answering poem" in the young poet. Kenneth Koch, in his wonderful book *Rose, Where Did You Get That Red?* suggests many ways for young people to respond to great poems. Any one of his exercises would undoubtedly work here—echoing the first line of a poem, posing a question similar to the question posed in a poem, answering that question, or making up a question of your own.

Marvin Bell, the first poet whose work appears in this book, has a poem called "Being in Love," which is about being in love, and about being in love *with* love. Being in love is something many seven-year-olds have already experienced. Being in love *with* love usually happens by the time you are twelve or thirteen. Writing love poems is hard work, but worth trying. So is writing a poem about how it feels to be in love. In another poem, Marvin Bell writes about someone who is not "beautiful, exactly" but "beautiful, inexactly." Readers could try writing a poem in honor of someone's imperfections. (Shakespeare did that, too, making fun of most love poems in his sonnet 18, "Shall I compare thee to a summer's day?")

Molly Bendall and Jane O. Wayne both have poems about listening in—eavesdropping—on other people. This is something young people do a lot, especially when their family is doing the talking, fighting, or whispering. Anyone can write an eavesdropping poem.

Robert Bly writes, "Well there's no end of things to do." It would be interesting to create a list of "things to do" the way he does in that poem, "Things My Brother and I Could Do." He ends another poem by saying "I have awakened at Missoula, Montana, utterly happy" ("In a Train"). When have we found ourselves suddenly "utterly happy"? That is a good subject for a poem.

So is a sleeping father, as in the poem by that title by David Chin. We've all watched our parents sleeping. He also writes about the class clown and outcast, in "Sterling Williams' Nosebleed." I have found that young people *always* have keen observations to make about the outcast children they have known.

I have included in this collection a prose poem by Vic Coccimiglio, and that is an interesting form for any poet to try. Suddenly you are free of line breaks, free of the need to feel you have to use a perfect rhythm or rhyme—though in fact, prose poems can use both, if they like.

Robert Creeley writes about what you might find if you pulled up the street and looked under it, about waiting for someone too long, about rain. All good subjects for poems.

Oscar Wilde once wrote, "Give a man a mask and he will tell you the truth." There are many ways to put on a mask in writing poetry. One way is to take on the voice, or *persona,* of someone else entirely. Another way is to write about somebody else: what they do, how they move or get ready to go to a dance on a Friday night. Cornelius Eady does this in his poem "Johnny Laces Up His Red Shoes." Ted Kooser does a similar thing in his poem "Myrtle," watching a woman deliver newspapers in the rain.

Martín Espada writes poems that are political—and so should we all, at least some of the time. There are so many injustices we should be writing about, looking at more closely. Then, too, he writes one poem, "Courthouse Graffiti for Two Voices" by simply recording graffiti he has seen. Anyone can "find" a poem—by writing down scraps of overheard conversation, or graffiti seen on a wall, or things found in a newspaper. How you arrange them becomes the poem.

Nikki Giovanni writes "the world is not a pleasant place to be without"—what? I would ask. We all have different answers. Each question triggers a new poem, a new answer.

Growing up, Andrew Hudgins used to ask himself what kind of tree he would like to be. One might well ask oneself, what kind of car would I want to be? What kind of weather? What kind of animal?

Galway Kinnell falls in love with the word "blackberry" in "Blackberry Eating," and David St. John with the word "guitar" in the poem called "Guitar." Poets often fall in love with the sound of certain words. They like to play with sounds. It would be good to write a poem in honor of that word, or simply playing with some favorite sounds, like "shh" or "sss" or what-have-you.

Maxine Kumin discovered that certain animals reminded her of people she had known in her life, and she wrote about that in "The Retrieval System." That's one of the most interesting ways to write about animals, though many people like to write about animals on any excuse at all. Gerald Stern writes about how it feels to touch a cow on the forehead, and how to behave when you see a dead animal on the road.

Years after the fact, Stanley Kunitz remembers a slap from his mother in his poem "The Portrait." We all have memories as stinging as slaps, and it's a relief to write them down in poem form.

Greg Kuzma's "Night Things" is a poem riddle. So is Linda Pastan's poem "Egg," and, in a subtle way, Maurya Simon's poem "Night." We all love riddles, so why not write one in the form of a poem, where people have to try to guess the thing you are describing? Often the title is the answer to the riddle. Other times, not. Emily Dickinson has written many poems like that—about a snake, a hummingbird, a broken heart, and God.

In "A Night in a World," Heather McHugh sees something "I wouldn't have known if I didn't stay home." "If not this, then not that" makes a good beginning for a poem, and so does "Because of this, that happened."

The last line of Diana Rivera's poem, "Dinner Together" provides the title for this book. The poem is an invitation—to the reader, and to a strange tiny creature who joins her for dinner. Poems are often invitations; you could try designing your own in poem form.

My own poem "Which One Is the Grown-up?" is a haiku—a Japanese poem form made up of seventeen syllables divided into three lines. The first line has five syllables; the second has seven; the third has five. I've found that young people love haiku, and write very beautifully in this form. Most haiku have a moment which is the wake-up call, the aha! upon which the whole poem turns. In the world's most famous haiku, this happens when a frog splashes into a pond. It doesn't give you much time or space, and yet in a haiku the whole world can enter in and wake us up.

Snow songs—like W. D. Snodgrass's poem by that title—are great things to write, especially on the day of the first snow. I never let that day go by without a poem. Someone who has never seen snow could look at a picture and try to imagine such a day.

Ruth Stone wrote a poem in honor of "The Nose." One could do the same for any part of the body.

Dieter Weslowski's poems are full of metaphors and images—apples hold "the light of their red lanterns," a tulip tree thrashing in wind looks like "a swimmer going under." You could try writing a poem loaded down with metaphors and similes—this is like that—one after the other, or writing a poem that is made entirely of images, those concrete details that call upon our senses to make us seem to see or smell or feel what the poet did at that moment. His poem "Pablo," is about how the Chilean poet Pablo Neruda found his desk. One might ask, what are *you* waiting to find and how are you going to find it? It's also a good excuse to go find a poem by Neruda, one of the greatest poets who ever lived.

Robley Wilson sends us off with his "Envoi"—a sort of farewell poem that often appears as the last poem of a book. Here it is used as the second to the last poem. Sylvia Plath wrote a similar poem once called "Valediction." Gerald Stern has a poem (not in this book) called "Waving Goodbye." We all find ways of saying farewell. I would end where this book began, what do you wish for when you wish "in the city of your heart"? Write and tell me, and I will answer. And long after that, the poem will answer for you.

LIZ ROSENBERG

BIOGRAPHICAL NOTES

MARVIN BELL grew up on the south shore of eastern Long Island and now lives in Iowa City, Iowa, and Port Townsend, Washington. He is the author of thirteen books of poetry and essays. He is married to Dorothy and they have two sons, Nathan and Jason.

MOLLY BENDALL's book *After Estrangement* was published in 1992 by Peregrine Smith Books. She teaches at the University of Southern California.

ROBERT BLY has been publishing poetry for the past thirty years. He has also published prose poems and translations and is the winner of many awards and honors, among them the National Book Award for *The Light Around the Body.* His book of tales and essays, *Iron John,* was a long-standing bestseller, and his newest book is *Sibling Society.* He lives most of the year in Minnesota.

DAVID CHIN grew up in Jersey City, New Jersey, attended public schools, Antioch College, Columbia University, and Binghamton University. He teaches creative writing and literature at Penn State University's Wilkes-Barre campus. His poems have appeared in various magazines and in a collection, *Chalked in Orange* (Mbirra Press).

VIC COCCIMIGLIO was born and raised in a working-class family in Pittsburgh, Pennsylvania. For the past seventeen years he has lived in southern California, where he has worked as a promotional writer. His poetry has appeared in literary magazines across the country as well as in *Strings: A Gathering of Family Poems* (Bradbury/MacMillan) and *Looking for Your Name* (Orchard Books).

ROBERT CREELEY has won countless awards and international honors for his many books of poetry, essays, and other writings. He holds the David Gray Chair in poetry at the State University of New York at Buffalo.

RITA DOVE was born in Akron, Ohio, in 1952. She has published six poetry collections, a short-story collection, a novel, a verse drama, and essays called *The Poet's World.* In 1987 she received the Pulitzer Prize for Poetry, and from 1993 to 1995 she served as Poet Laureate of the United States and consultant in poetry at the Library of Congress. She is Commonwealth Professor of

English at the University of Virginia and lives near Charlottesville with her husband and daughter.

CORNELIUS EADY is the author of four books of poems, including his newest, *You Don't Miss Your Water* (Henry Holt). His second book, *Victims of the Latest Dance Craze,* won the Lamont Poetry Prize in 1985, and he has also been a Guggenheim Fellow and a Rockefeller Foundation Fellow.

MARTÍN ESPADA was born in Brooklyn, New York, in 1957. He is the author of five books, most recently *City of Coughing and Dead Radiators* and *Imagine the Angels of Bread,* both from W. W. Norton. His awards include two National Endowment for the Arts Fellowships and the PEN/Revson Fellowship. A former tenant lawyer, he currently teaches at the University of Massachusetts at Amherst, where he lives with his wife, Katherine, and their son, Clemente.

TESS GALLAGHER is a poet, short-story writer, and essayist who writes in Sky House, the house she designed and built in her birthplace—Port Angeles, Washington. Her book of poetry *Moon Crossing Bridge* (Graywolf Press) was placed on the American Library Association's 1993 Most Notable Book List and won a Washington State Governor's Award in 1993.

MARIA MAZZIOTTI GILLAN is of working-class Italian American background. Her poetry books include *The Weather of Old Seasons, Taking Back My Name,* and *Where I Come From: Selected and New Poems.* She also edited, with her daughter Jennifer Gillan, *Unsettling America: Race and Ethnicity in Contemporary American Poetry* (Viking/Penguin). Gillan is the editor of *Footwork: The Paterson Literary Review* and director of the poetry center at Passaic County Community College in Paterson, New Jersey.

ALLEN GINSBERG was born in Newark, New Jersey, son of Naomi and the lyric poet Louis Ginsberg. His signal poem, "Howl," published in 1956, has been translated into more than twenty-two languages, and he has traveled to China, Russia, Scandinavia, and Eastern Europe, where he was crowned Prague May King in 1965. As a prolific poet, political activist, and cofounder of the Jack Kerouac School of Disembodied Poetics at the Naropa Institute, he has been a force in American life and literature for the past forty years.

Nikki Giovanni is the author of *Ego Tripping and Other Poems for the Young Reader; Spin a Soft Black Song;* and most recently, three books from Henry Holt: *Shimmy Shimmy Shimmy Like My Sister Kate: Looking at the Harlem Renaissance Through Poetry; The Genie in the Jar* (with illustrations by Chris Raschka); and *The Sun Is So Quiet* (with illustrations by Ashley Bryan). Her work has won her countless awards and honors.

Andrew Hudgins has published four books of poems. His first book was runner-up for the Pulitzer Prize, his second won the Poets' Prize, and the third was a finalist for the National Book Award. Andrew Hudgins writes: "Because my father was in the Air Force, we moved a lot. He retired in Montgomery, Alabama, where I went to high school and college. After college, I taught elementary school for a year, and then I bounced around for a long time, going to a lot of different graduate schools and doing a lot of different lousy jobs while I tried to learn how to write. Now I teach at the University of Cincinnati."

Milton Kessler writes: "My body is sixty-five years old now and has been writing poems since I was thirteen. A Rockaway Beach barnfire was the site of my first poem writing. I took time out from the night-games of my friends to stand by the fire and sing through writing. Suddenly it was ok to be different. 'A barnfire I will sing thee. . . .' I was a singer, a member of the select All City H. S. Chorus, in NYC, and met Eleanor Roosevelt because of it. I had the voice to be a professional singer but not the personality, and I continued with great choruses. *Vocal* human beauty and reality stayed extremely important to me. I sing all of my poems to my room or street or the clouds, out loud. When I think of my autobiography: asthma, singing, aloneness, dropping out, fire are the early memories.

"After college and into my teaching life, I wrote 'To Sing Was the Only Way Through,' a poem on my dropout high-school years. I'm amazed that I became a poet and college teacher. I didn't become famous but I've been around. My sixth collection of poems, *Riding First Car,* will be published soon. And in the summer of 1994, for the whole summer, my poem "Thanks Forever" was exhibited on the London subway.

"What have I been doing? Married for 43 years, have three adult children and one grandchild, Aaron. Teaching for almost 40 years, the last 30 at Bing-

199

hamton University, but also around the world. Each day is still full of amazement, aloneness, danger, and gratitude."

GALWAY KINNELL is the author of many books of poems, a novel, essays, and a children's book. His *Selected Poems* won the Pulitzer Prize and the American Book Award in 1982. He lives part of the time in New York City and part of the time in Vermont.

CAROLYN KIZER founded *Poetry Northwest* in 1959, served as the first literature program director at the National Endowment for the Arts, and presently lives in Sonoma, California. In 1985 she received the Pulitzer Prize for Poetry, and in 1988 was awarded the Theodore Roethke Prize. She has been poet-in-residence at many universities. Her three most recent poetry collections, *Carrying Over, Mermaids in the Basement,* and *The Nearness of You,* were published by Copper Canyon Press.

TED KOOSER's third book of poems is *Weather Central.* He makes his living as an executive for a life insurance company, and lives on an acreage near Garland, Nebraska.

MAXINE KUMIN has written ten books of poems and twenty books for children. Winner of the Pulitzer Prize and other honors, she lives on a farm in New Hampshire where she and her husband raise horses and vegetables.

STANLEY KUNITZ published his first book of poems, *Intellectual Things,* in 1930, when he was twenty-five. In 1995 he celebrated his ninetieth year with *Passing Through,* a collection of his later poems. "What is there left to confront," he has said, "but the great simplicities? I never tire of bird-song and sky and weather. I want to write poems that are natural, luminous, deep, spare. I dream of an art so transparent that you can look through and see the world."

Kunitz was born in Worcester, Massachusetts. The honors for his poetry include the Pulitzer Prize, the Bollingen Prize, the National Book Award, and the Brandeis Medal of Achievement. He has edited the Yale Series of Younger Poets, served as consultant in poetry to the Library of Congress, and taught for many years at Columbia University. For most of his adult life he has been active in the civil liberties and peace movements. Stanley Kunitz lives with his wife, the artist Elise Asher, in New York City and Provincetown on Cape Cod.

GREG KUZMA is the author of over twenty books of poems. His *Selected Poems* will be published by Carnegie Mellon University Press in 1996. He teaches poetry writing at the University of Nebraska in Lincoln.

LI-YOUNG LEE was born in 1957, in Jakarta, Indonesia, of Chinese heritage. Author of three books of poems and a memoir, he lives in Chicago with his wife and two children.

HEATHER MCHUGH has published a book of essays and five books of poems, including her most recent, *Hinge & Sign,* which was a National Book Award Finalist in 1994. She has also translated the work of Jean Follain and, with her husband, Niki Boris McHugh, collections of poems by Blaga Dimitrova and Paul Celan. She teaches at the University of Washington and is a visiting faculty member in the Master of Fine Arts program for writers at Warren Wilson College. She also lives part of the year in northern Maine.

KYOKO MORI was born in Kobe, Japan, in 1957. She has lived in the American Midwest since 1977. Her books are *Fallout* (poems) published by Tia Chacha Press, *Shizuko's Daughter* and *One Bird* (novels), and *The Dream of Water* (memoir) from Henry Holt. She lives in Green Bay, Wisconsin, and teaches at St. Norbert College.

SHARON OLDS was born in San Francisco, in 1942, and attended Stanford University and Columbia University. *The Wellspring,* her fifth collection, was published by Knopf in January 1996. Her other books are *The Father, The Gold Cell, Satan Says,* and *The Dead and the Living,* which was chosen as the Lamont Poetry Selection by the Academy of American Poets and received the National Book Critics Circle Award. Ms. Olds teaches in the graduate creative writing program at New York University, and for twelve years has helped run a writing workshop at the Sigismund Goldwater Memorial Hospital, a public hospital for the severely physically disabled.

LINDA PASTAN was born in New York City, graduated from Radcliffe College in 1954, received a Master of Arts from Brandeis University in 1957. She has published nine volumes of poetry, including the most recent, *An Early Afterlife.* She has won the Dylan Thomas Award, a Pushcart Prize, the Di Castagnbola Award, the Bess Hokin Prize, and the Maurice English Award. In 1991 she was appointed Poet Laureate of Maryland and served till January 1995.

DIANA RIVERA, a poet and painter, was born and raised in Puerto Rico and has lived in the United States since the 1970s. She is the author of *Bird Language* (Bilingual Press), and her poems have appeared in several anthologies, including *Paper Dance, 55 Latino Poets* (Persea Press) and *The Woman That I Am* (St. Martin's Press). She has exhibited her paintings throughout the United States and Puerto Rico.

LIZ ROSENBERG grew up on the north shore of Long Island. She has published four books of poems, the most recent of which is *Children of Paradise* (University of Pittsburgh Press), and many books for children, including *Monster Mama,* illustrated by Stephen Gammell; *The Carousel,* illustrated by Jim LaMarche; and the book you are reading now. She teaches at Binghamton University in Binghamton, NY, where she lives with her husband, David, and their son, Eli. They spend parts of the year near the water in Florida and Cape Cod.

DAVID ST. JOHN is the author of five collections of poetry, most recently *Study for the World's Body: New and Selected Poems* (HarperCollins), which was nominated for the National Book Award in Poetry. He has recently published a book of essays, reviews, and interviews, *Where the Angels Come Toward Us* (White Pine Press) and won the Prix de Rome in 1984. He is professor of English at the University of Southern California.

MAURYA SIMON was born in 1950 in New York City. She is the author of five books of poetry, most recently *The Golden Labyrinth* (University of Missouri Press). She teaches in the creative writing program at the University of California, Riverside.

W. D. SNODGRASS just retired from teaching, and has recently finished *The Fuehrer Bunker*—a cycle of poems he has been working on for thirty-five years. His many books of poems have won numerous awards and honors.

GERALD STERN is the author of ten books of poetry, including *Leaving Another Kingdom: Selected Poems.* He recently retired from teaching at the Writer's Workshop in Iowa, and now lives in Easton, Pennsylvania. His newest book is *Odd Mercy* (Norton).

RUTH STONE has been a Guggenheim Fellow and a member of the Radcliffe Institute. She has received the Delmore Schwartz Award for Poetry and a

Whiting Writer's Award. Her newest book of poems is *Simplicity,* published by Paris Press. She teaches creative writing at Binghamton University, and spends summers in Vermont.

LUCIEN STRYK has published more than thirty books, including *The Penguin Book of Zen Poetry* (Penguin Books, London), *Collected Poems 1953–1983* (Ohio University Press/Swallow Press), and *Of Love and Barley: Haiku of Basho* (Penguin). He has won numerous awards and honors: a Ford Foundation Fellowship, a National Endowment for the Arts Fellowship, Illinois Author of the Year, and others.

ALICE WALKER is a poet, novelist, short-story writer, essayist, and biographer. Her published work includes two collections of short stories, four volumes of poetry, two collections of essays, two children's books, a biography of Langston Hughes, and five novels, including *The Color Purple* for which she won the Pulitzer Prize and the American Book Award for fiction. Alice Walker was born in Eatonton, Georgia, in 1944 and received her B.A. from Sarah Lawrence College in 1965. She currently lives in northern California.

JANE O. WAYNE's collection of poems, *Looking Both Ways,* received the 1985 Devins Award. Her work has appeared in many publications, and received first prize from *Yankee Magazine* in 1988.

DIETER WESLOWSKI writes: "I was born in Düsseldorf, Germany, in 1950. Since then, I have lived in Spain and the United States, found my mother after forty years of separation; and published two books of verse, *The Bird Who Steals Everything Shining* (MSS Press) and *Candles of Wheat* (Black Tie Press)."

ROBLEY WILSON has published books of poetry and fiction (University of Pittsburgh Press) and is editor of the *North American Review.* He teaches English at the University of Northern Iowa.

203

Page 110: Greg Kuzma, young. Courtesy of author; Greg Kuzma, adult. Courtesy of author.

Page 114: Li-Young Lee, young. Courtesy of author; Li-Young Lee, adult. Courtesy of author.

Page 118: Heather McHugh, 1950. Courtesy of author; Heather McHugh (left) and Bryan Gardner. Photo by Greg Bliss.

Page 122: Kyoko Mori (center). Courtesy of author; Kyoko Mori, adult. Courtesy of author.

Page 126: Sharon Olds, young. Courtesy of author; Sharon Olds, adult. Photo copyright © David Bartolomi.

Page 132: Linda Pastan, young. Photo by Peilie Photographers. Courtesy of author; Linda Pastan, adult. Photo copyright © Goodman/Van Riper. Courtesy of author.

Page 136: Diana Rivera, age 2. Courtesy of author; Diana Rivera, adult. Courtesy of author.

Page 142: Liz Rosenberg, age 10–11. Courtesy of author; Liz Rosenberg, adult. Courtesy of author.

Page 146: David St. John, young. Courtesy of author; David St. John, adult. Photo by Rex Wilder.

Page 150: Maurya Simon, young. Courtesy of author; Maurya Simon, adult. Courtesy of author.

Page 154: W. D. Snodgrass, young. Courtesy of author; W. D. Snodgrass, adult. Photo by Kathleen Snodgrass.

Page 158: Gerald Stern (right) with sister. Courtesy of author; Gerald Stern, adult. Photo copyright © 1994 Maring J. Desht.

Page 164: Ruth Stone, young. Courtesy of author; Ruth Stone, adult. Courtesy of author.

Page 168: Lucien Stryk, young, age 3 in Poland. Courtesy of author; Lucien Stryk, adult. Courtesy of author.

Page 172: Alice Walker, age 6. Courtesy of author; Alice Walker, adult. Photo by Jean Weisinger, 1991. Courtesy of Harcourt Brace Jovanovich.

Page 176: Jane O. Wayne, young. Courtesy of author; Jane O. Wayne, adult. Courtesy of author.

Page 182: Dieter Weslowski, age 10. Courtesy of author; Dieter Weslowski, adult. Photo by Jim Quinnan.

Page 186: Robley Wilson, age 2. Courtesy of author; Robley Wilson, adult. Photo by Sidney Sander.

INDEX OF FIRST LINES

All night the sound had come back again, 40

As a boy, I'd still have asked why Jack must spend exactly two dollars at the corner store, 124

As I wandered on the beach I saw the heron standing, 94

At sixteen, I worked after high school hours at a printing plant, 56

Because I brought him here I hold his hand, 178

Because I'd seen a man thrust his straight fingers through a melon, 78

Being in love with someone who is not in love with you, 8

By accident, I gaze at these two young guys, 51

Dear waves, what will you do for me this year?, 162

Everyone complains about the nose, 166

Five a.m., and I've been up for hours, 170

For hours I sat on our driveway beneath the dogwood tree, 34

For instance, the child skipping is not touching the earth at all, 144

Hard? You don't know what hard is, boy, 76

I could just as easily be nine years old, 35

I'd like to be a tree, 77

If Fred Astaire had been really smart, 49

If you watch me picking stones out of these red lentils, 180

I have always loved the word *guitar*, 148

I like it here, under the apple tree, 138

I love to go out in late September, 88

In New Jersey once, marigolds grew wild, 64

In the evening haze darkening on the hills, 89

In the steamer is the trout, 116

In this kingdom the sun never sets, 134

I pulled the street up as you suggested, 38

It begins with my dog, now dead, who all his long life carried about in his head the brown eyes of my father, 102

I too am waiting for the sea, 185

it rained in my sleep, 135

It started about noon. On top of Mount Batte, 22

It would be worth it to go ninety miles out of your way, 160

I waited too long, 39

I was one of the saved, 23

I went to the field to break and to bury my precious things, 60

I wish in the city of your heart, 189

I wouldn't have known if I didn't stay home, 120

Jimmy C. Greatest Car Thief Alive, 54

Maybe she does her homework the way she does her chores, 181

My father sits in his chair and snores, 28

My mother never forgave my father for killing himself, 106

my old druid, winter is here, 185

Now, as the stars unfleece themselves, 152

Off go the crows from the roof, 48

Oh God, God!—Calm down, 144

Once when the moon was out about three-quarters, 13
one. now another. one more, 156
One afternoon in her loft the girl reaches in the closet for her huaraches, 19
O three-toned green little place with trees, 82

Pigeons shake their wings on the copper church roof, 68

Reading in Li Po how "the peach blossom follows the water," 107
Remember me?, 174

She begins, and my grandmother joins her, 117
Sitting by the barbecue waiting for sausages and hot dogs, 141
Sometimes the weather goes on for days, 12
So the milk carton which used to wobble on the little metal desk will no longer arrive, 145
Sterling Williams has a nosebleed, 29
Sun in the mouth of the day, 188

Ten rains, and then snow, then more snow, 113
That evening, after Scotty and his mother moved out, 184

That small girl crouched on the top steps, 179
That sound of his is like a boat with black sails, 25
The broader leaves collect enough to see early, 9
There has been a light snow, 25
The wind has all its answers in a sock, 112
the world is not a pleasant place to be, 72

Wearing her yellow rubber slicker, 98
Well there's no end of things to do, 24
When I got there the dead opossum looked like an enormous baby sleeping on the road, 161
When I got to the airport I rushed up to the desk, 129
When the sun shuts down her cantina the lizard goes underground, 184
Who I am is a short person with small feet and fingers, 11
With the storm moved on the next town, 44

"Yes, Your Honor, there are rodents," 55
You are not beautiful, exactly, 10
You might have been a meadowlark making your way over winter's blue fields, 153